PENGUIN F

SIX SATURDAYS OF
OTHER ESSAYS

Ferdinand Pisigan Jarin is one of the Philippines' foremost author and creative nonfictionist. He is the author of *Six Saturdays of Beyblade and other Essays* (originally *Anim na Sabado ng Beyblade at Iba Pang Sanaysay*), which won a National Book Award for Best Book of Nonfiction in Filipino in 2014 from the Manila Critics Circle and National Book Development Board and was a finalist for Madrigal-Gonzales First Best Book Award administered by the University of the Philippines Institute of Creative Writing (UP ICW). The book, since its first edition up to the present, is a consistent bestseller for creative nonfiction in Filipino. Its main story, the *Six Saturdays of Beyblade* is one of the mandatory readings for the Philippines' secondary students studying Philippine and Asian Literature. Jarin is a three-time Don Carlos Palanca Memorial Awardee for Literature, the Philippines' most prestigious literary award-giving body. Jarin is teaching Filipino Language and Creative Writing at the Division of Humanities of the College of Arts and Sciences, University of the Philippines Visayas.

John Toledo is an emerging author, translator, and creative nonfictionist from the Philippines. He translated to English the Filipino original of the *Six Saturdays of Beyblade* and it was first published in the winter issue of the *Asymptote Journal* (2021). He currently writes criticism and essays about Philippine literature and pop culture in both Filipino and English. A graduate of the Filipino creative writing program at the University of the Philippines Diliman, Toledo teaches Filipino language, Philippine and World Literature and Creative Writing in various universities in the Philippines. *Six Saturdays of Beyblade* is his first book of translation.

Six Saturdays of Beyblade and Other Essays

Ferdinand Pisigan Jarin

Translated by John Leihmar C. Toledo

PENGUIN BOOKS

An imprint of Penguin Random House

PENGUIN BOOKS

USA | Canada | UK | Ireland | Australia
New Zealand | India | South Africa | China | Southeast Asia

Penguin Books is part of the Penguin Random House group of companies
whose addresses can be found at global.penguinrandomhouse.com

Published by Penguin Random House SEA Pte Ltd
9, Changi South Street 3, Level 08-01,
Singapore 486361

First published in Penguin Books by Penguin Random House SEA 2023

ISBN 9789815058994

Typeset in Calson by MAP Systems, Bengaluru, India

www.penguin.sg

Contents

Preface

Like a patient etherized upon a table, I wrote

I had a strong feeling that because I was still numb by my son's death, I suddenly went into writer-mode in the first evening of his wake. I was able to conceptualize immediately how to write the story of my son's life and death. The title itself 'Six Saturdays of Beyblade' immediately came to mind because right from the start, I was counting each Saturday my son and I met before his passing, especially after he started to get sick. His last six Saturdays were the heaviest for me.

I was numb because even if the pain of his early death consumed my heart, I had to pull myself together as a father because I had to take care of his remains—from bringing his body to the morgue, choosing his casket, finding a place for his wake, etc. I remember computing what I'll spend on the things I had to place on his casket while his body was placed in a room where he would be embalmed inside a funeral parlour in Makati. I heard it's closed now and was replaced by a private elementary school.

What added to this lingering numbness back then was the constant arrival of friends, neighbours, relatives, colleagues, and students who paid their respects. I had to attend to them, talk to them, thank them, and tell stories about how we found out about Rebo's leukemia, from the struggles we experienced to extend his life until the day he was gone. I didn't include in the story were those days I borrowed money from many people and queued up at government agencies for cash aids. But the one thing I won't forget that motivated me to write the essay was our experiences inside the hospital. I was motivated to expose the already grim state of health service in our country. Making him alive in the hearts and minds of my present and future readers was secondary to this higher purpose.

After he was buried, the days of longing and numbness eventually subsided. Once I got back to my rented apartment after the funeral, I broke into the most painful cry while tightly hugging his photograph. Weeks had passed by when I decided to write his story. It was not because I was ready to write. I just felt that I may not write it well and truthfully if I waited for this pain in my chest to pass. Or, if the time came when we had moved on from his absence, I may not want to write it anymore.

I wrote the story with a pen and on a sheet of paper. It was the first time I wrote without erasing. Words flowed with certainty. It was also the first time that I wrote without leaving the seat. I remember writing the essay at four o'clock in the afternoon and stopping at three in the morning. It was the first time I sat down and wrote like that for a long time because there were many instances where I had to pause writing in the middle of a page to weep. My writing tended to be slow because every now and then I would wipe the tears from the papers on the table.

Similar to the process of writing 'Six Saturdays of Beyblade', all the essays in this collection are written in my natural voice, striking conversations with an imaginary stranger willing to listen. My close friends observed that when I would strike a conversation with them, I'd often persuade them of my beliefs. When I don't use the thick tones of my arguments, the words become music to their ears. So I thought, why not use this kind of tone in writing my stories? It was also my dream that my readers discover who they are in each of my essays. I want to convince them that my stories, albeit very personal, are their stories too. Would I still burden my readers with heavy storytelling when, in fact, these stories themselves carry their own weights? Most of all, I preferred showing more emotional truths in each story.

I didn't burden myself with writing after the style that is popular today in literature. The truth is, I don't care about those styles. That's why some readers and critics point out that I didn't have a single way of writing. Here is a funny story: I was once accused by fake critics that my essay collection was written by many writers. That it wasn't really originally mine and I commissioned some friends as ghost writers. Maybe that's why these bashers have no careers and names in the field of literature because they are the kinds of fools who offer a loose-canon type of criticism.

All stories and forms of storytelling in this collection were the fruits of the mature sensibilities I developed since childhood. How these sensibilities shaped my heart and mind to tell stories and choose the stories that are worth sharing on the page. The motivation is not to please the literati of the academe. Not even the panelists in writing workshops. My sensibilities in writing were further developed by reading and marrying my personal narrative to the people, streets, towns and homelands, to the discourses of my time and my society.

May you read well and know yourself.

When will you write your story too?

9 August 2022   Ferdinand Pisigan Jarin
                                                   The Courtyards, Baguio City,
                                                                 Philippines

Homecoming

It was raining hard that night and the howls of stray dogs echoed across the village. What I remember from those scenes come as passing memories and some tattered threads of thought that I have to stitch up somewhere in my mind. I remember hugging Mama's legs tightly while watching her in a shouting match with the landlord of our rented house. Tears poured down our cheeks as the heavy raindrops continued falling on our doorstep. It was only then that I realized that we were all crying—Mama and me outside, and my younger brother Michael inside our house. I was three years old and my brother was one. I knew we were being evicted that night, and I felt very powerless. The memory is as clear as water. It all happened at Ipil Street in Cembo, Makati.

My father left us long before that unforgettable evening. He went back to his first family and wife. Mama, who was in a live-in relationship with him, didn't know that my father was a married man then. It all led us to this moment. Because Mama couldn't pay the rent, we were forced to leave. That night, she decided to go home to the province. We left at once and brought with us the hope to see the light of another day.

The next morning, we were at the house of Tatay and Nanay, my mother's parents.

This place is called Quinabuangan. Even today, I don't know where its name came from or what it means. Sitio

Quinabuangan, Poblacion, Candelaria, Zambales is its long official name. Because it had the word 'poblacion' in its name, it was a part of the town. Most days, I called it a district-town.

Quinabuangan is not within the geographic boundary of the pueblo. Most towns in this province look similar—arranged within a circle, the municipal hall, the church, the market and the schools facing each other. In the middle of the circle is the plaza where you'll find small or big grassy parks where a tall statue of Dr Jose Rizal stood. It is surrounded by large Spanish ancestral houses on the sides of these streets—some of these houses were later remodeled to a modern design—which are owned by people belonging to noble classes or affluent families of the hacienderos and professionals.

If you walk along the cemented road from the plaza, about 500 metres to the left, you'll find Quinabuangan. Different structures facing each other surround it. There are lots of mango, tamarind, and other fruit-bearing trees along the way. As you enter inside, you will see to the right a farmland divided in the middle by Zambales' national highway. To the left is a river that flows to other barrios of Candelaria. Beyond is the town's cemetery. In the middle are the townsfolk's households where not more than a hundred people live. Most of the people here make a living in Quinabuangan by farming, fishing, cultivating trees, and selling tamarind and mangoes.

A year later, after we left the city, Mama decided to go back to Manila and look for a job. It was time for me to start studying in school. She was lucky because she was immediately hired by a sewing factory near Mandaluyong City. She left us temporarily in the care of our grandparents.

I felt the heaviness of the situation even though I was still young back then. Every time my mother left us in the middle of the night, me and my brother would cry in agony sitting at the windows of our house. Later on, Mama found a way to sneak out of the house while we were still asleep. She didn't know that it hurt me so much even if I did not cry when I woke up. I'd run as fast outside our front yard and stare at the street corner of Quinabuangan where I'd see the main road and wait for the Victory Liners to pass by, imagining that they would probably bring my mother home. I always prayed for my mother to change her mind in the middle of the ride and return to us so we'd be together again. That she would stay a few more days with us. Even if we didn't eat. Even if I didn't go to school. Just the three of us together. Even without a father. Yet her sudden return never happened. That's when the tears would start rolling down my cheeks and I would mope under the shade of our guava tree. Sometimes, I'd go back to sleep beside Michael, caress his hair, and accept that it would be the two of us left in this place again.

We were not well-off like the other families in Quinabuangan. That's why Michael and I had an assigned chore in our grandparent's house. We'd get water, cook rice, pick up pieces of firewood for cooking, and buy food from the market. We'd join our cousins and uncles to go fishing, or we'd do some crabbing by the river using our feet. Uncle Jun and Uncle Genie would sometimes do the *mangingilaw*, which is what they referred to as catching tons of fish and crabs in the evening at Quinabuangan. They would wake us up in the wee hours of the morning to boast of their catch and sometimes we would dress the wounds they got. If there was no catch at all, we'd eat *monamon*—anchovies called dilis in Manila, stewed in mangoes and bagoóng. It is also made as a kilawin, served as a dish in drinking sprees. Sometimes we would eat small fishes called *terong*. Some believe them to be yellow tail fusilier fish because of their similar red underside and shape. Like the *monamon*, the *terong* was also stewed in mangoes and bagoóng.

For most of my life in elementary school, I stayed in Candelaria. I remember being the shortest kid in class, always in front of the line during the flag ceremony. I was often ordered by the taller kids to get the ball if it was thrown beyond the fence—because these larger kids couldn't pass through the holes—and often I was bullied by those larger than me. Sometimes I'd be the sidekick of a bigger classmate who had a big enemy too. That big enemy would also have a sidekick.

The people that I'd often tell stories to and be friends with were those who were short like me—classmates or schoolmates alike. But it wasn't just being small in size that made me feel small back then. I was small also because I was not wealthy like my classmates who were the grandchildren of some politician, professional, inheritor of large tracts of farmland, or owner of businesses in Candelaria or Manila. Such people lived in large houses in Candelaria.

Meanwhile, I'd go to school wearing anything as long as it was clean. Back in those days, we didn't have uniforms. Sometimes, Mama would get us clothes from Manila. My favourite design was the Ghostbusters bag and shirt that Michael and I both wore to school. But more often I wore cheap clothes. There were times when I endured wearing a worn-out pair of rubber shoes in school. It was a hand-me-down from Uncle Genie. My classmates would tease that my shoes would always smile to show its teeth, meaning my little toes inside. I'd secretly cry after class while walking home to Quinabuangan. In these unfortunate moments of my life, I didn't join the other kids going home so that no one would see the tears falling down on my face.

Most of the time I didn't have money to buy food, so during recess break I'd just read and read lots of books. Sometimes when I couldn't resist the pangs of hunger, I would beg for food from my classmates. Some of them would share their lunch and some wouldn't. Fortunately, in my last few years at elementary school, the nutribun—a bread distributed by USAID—and klim, a milk named after a milk brand with a similar name, became popular. It was cheap, so I could buy it. It saved me from starving every recess. I was able to hide the shame I felt every time I begged for food from my classmates. Somehow, when I bought these foods, I felt taller.

I'd always go home carrying my bag with wheels on my head. It was too big and heavy for my small, lanky body. When I reached Quinabuangan, I'd walk faster. Then, I'd put down my bag on the floor, take a bath—there were times when I forgot— light the firewood for the stove, boil the rice, and run under the big mango tree or to the rice field where me and my childhood friends would play hide and seek, patintero, tag, mango-picking races, fist fights, banter, boast, cry, take sides, and fall down. The rice field and the large mango tree became our little plaza. My favourite game was the 'it-it', which happened at night especially when there was a wake in our barrio. Children would divide in two groups. One group was the 'it' and they would seek the hiders. Every member caught in their hideouts will be shouted with 'it!' When all of my friends were caught, it would be their turn to be the 'it' and they would seek while the others hid. It took a long time to look for the hiders. Often, me and my cousins would go home past the curfew our Nanay set for us. The next day, we would hear the sermons from our grandparents and if we were unlucky, we'd get a beating. But if it was Tatay, our grandpa, who hissed at us from the corner of our front yard, it was heard across Quinabuangan. Once we heard it, be it afternoon or evening, we would end the game and go home immediately. The last seeker would always be pissed off because he'd be the last to know that we're gone.

When I was in Grade 5, Mama took Michael to Manila for good. I was left alone in Quinabuangan to finish elementary school. I was sad constantly because I missed my brother, even if at times we fought or didn't get along. There were times when I'd stare at the picture of Manila's Luneta Park in my textbook just to imagine what he might be seeing there. I dreamt of reuniting with him in Manila. There were a lot of questions on my mind. Who protected him there when somebody pranked him like I did in Quinabuangan? Did he think of me sometimes? After I returned from school, my feet would feel too heavy to play games because I was so lonely. I wanted to hear my brother's laughter again. Our banter. Our horse-playing and teasing on the bed. But most of all, I missed having him as a brother in that place.

A year passed by and after my graduation from elementary school, Mama decided I should transfer to Manila so I could go to high school. I would have to leave my grandparents in Quinabuangan for good.

I left this place in the wee hours of the morning, after my graduation day from elementary school in Candelaria. I was that kid, excited for my new life in Manila, and never looked back to Quinabuangan. However, I was always searching for something.

The time came when all of us were gone from Quinabuangan. Nanay and Tatay were petitioned by my aunts living in the United States. All of us by then were now living in Manila. The house was abandoned. I imagined it missing its previous owners. The grass rose and the plants crawled. The mangoes, star apples, guavas, and tamarind pods hanging from the trees would have rotted. But it was not for long. My grandparents didn't survive the cold weather abroad and returned to Quinabuangan. They chose to spend their remaining days caring for this place they loved.

It was 1995 when Nanay died of complications from many illnesses. Six years later, Tatay followed. He died of old age and depression after Nanay's death. The only time I was able to go home was during their wake and burial in Quinabuangan. It was a return for an instant. I was brought down by heavy emotions at my Lolo and Lola's loss, but I did not let this show. Moreover, I felt the need to leave the place immediately. I saw our house as a sad place, and Quinabuangan, a lonely town. After their deaths, aside from some invitations as a guest-speaker in my elementary school, I didn't visit there for many years.

It was only when a cousin, who grew up with me in Nanay and Tatay's house, and died from a severe illness that I came home to Quinabuangan. I was with Michael then. My classmates and childhood friends would say over drinks that I would return to Quinabuangan only when somebody died in the family. I said it was merely a coincidence. Deep inside, I knew that coming home was searching for a deeper part of my humanity.

All roads leading to Quinabuangan are now cemented. The giant mango trees are gone. The place where the trees stood tall is covered in cement and now a basketball court. The land that used to be a rice field is now covered with houses of concrete. Our house, which once had a basement made of cement and nipa leaves, is now a one-storey, concrete semi-bungalow. Also, the mango trees in our front yard are gone. What remains is the stump of my favourite guava tree.

During drinking nights, I savoured the scent of soil and gluttonized on Indian mangoes and *terong*. Once the alcohol kicked in, I saw again the faces of my cousins and childhood friends when we were young. Those who were still here and those who were gone. We were playing at the rice field and under the mango tree, seeking and hiding everywhere just to win the 'it-it.' There was no more roughhousing or teasing. No more boasting or showing off. It was all games and children laughing at each other.

From the street corner, I saw little Ferdie, that kid carrying a bag with wheels on his head, wearing his worn-out shoes, smiling and hurrying in his footsteps to go home. Excited to enter the house and pay his respect to his grandparents. Put down his bag. Take a bath. Fire up the wood on the stove. Boil the rice. Play. And at night, before sleeping, look out the window, imagine his mother and his brother, and stare at the starry skies of Quinabuangan and dream, and dream.

D' Pol Pisigan Band

It was the summer vacation before Grade 5 when Tatay bequeathed to all of us his music, our only inheritance. The trumpet was ready upstairs, waiting for us, while we panted and wiped our sweats from playing in the rice field. The solfege was neatly placed on the music sheet stand. Facing it was a seat without a backrest. Our rehearsal space was a large room, the bedrooms of Tatay's children and grandchildren. It was one of the two rooms on the second floor. The other small room was for Nanay and Tatay.

Our walls were thatched with nipa leaves. The floor upstairs was made of bamboo—where we would often secretly insert our uncircumcised penises to pee so we wouldn't have to go downstairs in the middle of the night. Though the bamboo poles were very close to each other, some gaps were left deliberately that looked into our basement, which served as a storage room for instruments and firewood. Downstairs, the house was walled and paved with cement. The architecture of our house in Quinabuangan was a fusion of antique and modern materials in construction. It was a contrasting image of a shanty house, above was 'dirt-poor' and below was the 'occasionally well-off'.

It was in this house where my Tatay's music filled our innocence and adolescence.

The bamboo on the floor creaked from the weight of our feet. Cousin Rowel, cousin Chris, my younger brother Michael,

Of course, I'd say these were the opposite of what our band did, especially if one went back to how it started. It could be said that it was a labour of sweat and love.

Tatay and Nanay arrived in Candelaria as a newly wedded couple. There were fourteen towns in Zambales including Candelaria. In these towns, there was a mixed number of speakers in the Sambal and Ilokano languages. Nanay had lots of relatives in this town while Tatay was considered the newcomer. He was born in Calamba, Laguna, and she came from Subic. They met at an American military base in Olongapo. He was a musician, playing the trombone in a combo. I didn't know the exact details but the story was that Nanay was able to meet Tatay because she was interested in music. I am pretty sure the performer and the spectator stared at each other the whole night! From that evening, all the elements of their love for each other emerged and combined, strengthened by the music. They decided to settle at Pamibian, a barrio in Candelaria, but it was only for a short time because they found a better and larger piece of land at Quinabuangan. Love speaks in different ways. From his awakening to his adolescence in Calamba and Manila, Tatay brought his trombone and love in Candelaria, Zambales, to be the husband of Florentina and a father to their ten children.

They were known here as the couple, Poling and Floring. He became acquainted with some of the farmers and fisher folk as an elementary music teacher at the town's public school. They later on became his friends as they grew up and eventually, became his bandmates. From handling the sickle and the fishing net, Tatay taught Lolo Handring, Hemin, Pilo, Aloy, Mino, Tanny, Daming, and Deoning every afternoon to blow the trumpet, saxophone, and flute; play the drums and crash the cymbals; identify the pitch; keep up with the tempo; and recognize the melodies of chacha, balse, rumba, kundiman, disco, and other styles. During these times, Tatay also learnt how to speak Sambal, and it didn't take long for him to organize his band. Since then, especially on Saturdays and Sundays when he didn't have classes, he was always invited to play music at local gatherings like birthdays, weddings, baptisms, and often, the last evenings of a wake and a funeral. Every summer vacation, the marching band would fill the streets with their vibrancy at the fiesta. Tatay would start early in the morning. They would march around the whole barrio to wake up the townsfolk and mark the beginning of the fiesta. And for the rest of the day, they would perform music in the parade, from the people's gathering to the evening procession of the patron saint that ended the celebration.

Almost all of the men in our family became band members. First were our uncles, then grandchildren. I have heard stories that my father taught four of my uncles to play the saxophone and trumpet. But they weren't able to finish their rehearsals. Uncle Jun chose to play the guitar and the drums. He laid down the trumpet and performed at the beer houses and night clubs in the neighbouring towns of Masinloc and Santa Cruz, until he eventually settled in Olongapo. He became the vocalist and leader of different bands, playing to the beats of a variety, from standard, slow rock, Pinoy Rock, to disco. Meanwhile, Uncle Genie quickly 'fell in love'. After laying down the trumpets, he immediately left to find his passion in Manila and strum his own guitar compositions, which were love songs and sentimental music. He often named his songs after the names of his girlfriends or the girls he was courting. His audience were his buddies on drinking nights. Uncle Ciel was the fiercest and got married in Manila. The eldest among the boys, Uncle Boy, got married earlier before the birth of Uncle Genie. All of them, after blowing a few notes on the trumpet, finally left the band to live their own lives. The six daughters of Tatay and Nanay—including my mother—also knew how to sing and play the guitar and piano. Like my uncles, they found interest in other places—studying and love. That's why Tatay's expectation for me as his grandson, who would soon continue what he started, was so high. I am his last card, as the saying goes. The expectation was heavier than the trumpet I carried.

Every time we performed, Tatay entrusted me with the drums—tom-tom or snare—or the cymbals because I wasn't yet done studying the trumpet. He didn't want me to train by the ear. The teenage sons of his original bandmates learnt music earlier than me even though they were only trained by ear. This is because my uncles were enchanted by the guitar, love, and rock-and-roll, and pulled them away for good! The time came, when I was the only relative left in the band, but the teenage sons would often order me—and surreptitiously give a knuckle blow on my head if I didn't obey—to buy them cigarettes during rehearsal breaks. Because I was the youngest, I was often pranked by these fools. To the old, I was their protégé, the youngest musician. For the teenage boys, I was their servant boy and the kid they'd bully and quickly pull the pants off of.

My favourite instrument was the cymbals. I could clash the cymbals brilliantly especially when we played chacha tunes like 'Gracela' and 'Cherry Pink'. These songs would truly make me dance to the beats. There were many parts in this piece that permitted solo parts for the drums and the cymbals. And surely everyone who would hear them, on any occasion, would dance and get a dancing partner with them. In the middle of the piece, I would give my all in clashing the cymbals. There were times when I would clash, glide, and spin the cymbals, then quickly throw them mid-air and catch the right cymbal before clashing it with the left one. I would often do this exhibition when we'd perform in barrios or houses where my school crushes live.

Or perhaps a beautiful maiden of my age was in the crowd. Before I performed, I would gaze at them. After the performance, I'd try to look again at them but most of the time, no one flirted back. I was the only one looking. Showing off. Unnoticed. However, when I played the cymbals, I would feel myself growing a few inches taller especially when I played the music that made me an equal to the older musicians because I was very sure that the children my age didn't know this feeling.

Our band's uniform was white shirt and black pants. When we accepted a contract to perform, Nanay, my grandmother, would neatly iron the clothes the night before the performance. In the early morning, one-by-one, members from neighbouring towns, taken by a rented car. We were the last ones to reach—a privilege of Tatay's as the bandleader. Whatever town or barrio our destinations was at, it was sure that our band would show their talent the moment we stepped on the floor. If it was a wake, the band arrived in the house of the bereaved on the last evening of the wake. We played different pieces. We began with the sad ones like the kundiman, or contemporary love songs and break up songs. As we played far into the night, and the grieving became obsessed with the spirits of socializing and alcohol, the band played dancing tunes.

Some of my favourites were the boogie 'Go, Johnny, Go' and the slow romantic waltz 'Let Me Call You Sweetheart.' CDs, karaoke, videoke, and iPod weren't invented yet, and our band served as the biggest live concert to the people of the province. It was here that they would often emotionally request their favourite songs, which Tatay would immediately command us to find the tune of, especially the pieces we hadn't rehearsed. Often somebody would join in singing or dancing to our music. Often, we'd stop in the middle of the song and carry our instruments if a drunk stud suddenly shouted and challenged the people in a boxing match.

In my young mind, this was the thing I didn't want to see like the times when I couldn't force myself to eat anything served at a wake except candies and the biscuits. I would be paranoid that the meat served came from the innards and body parts of the dead. There was a time I couldn't forget the face of the dead person I saw inside the casket. This happened when the band was resting. Yolanda was her name. I forget her surname. When I read her name on the plaque beside the casket and looked at her picture from when she was still alive, I was scared out of my wits because of how swollen and different her face was. It seemed like she was hollow and wide inside from the embalming.

I left that wake with the image of her face still on my mind, and I wasn't able to sleep for many nights. In fact, I am still frightened of peeking inside caskets and avoid this by inviting somebody to chat and drink with me.

I also had an encounter with a white lady who was staring at the sky one late evening while the band was walking home. I am not sure if this was caused by my over-active imagination. Up to this day, I can still remember the details of the woman's appearance. I was at the end of that marching band when without a word, I ran as fast as I could and reached those in the front. The next day, before we started the funeral procession, my encounter with the ghost was the butt of the joke and the stuff of conversation among the members, including Tatay.

Prak-prak. Prak-prak. Parararaaaaaak. Prak-prak. The strike of the snare marked a finished set and the signal that a new set was being prepared to be played. This strike served as a temporary rest, where players wiped the saliva filled inside the mouthpiece of the wind instruments, and the percussionists rested their hands for a while. We did all of these things while marching in the middle of the streets every fiesta or when we accompanied the dead to the church and cemetery. We often had two-to-three sets of pieces in our repertoire that had five-to-seven songs in each set. It depended on the size of the town and the length of the main road. It depended on how far the house was from the church or cemetery. Even back then, though my body was that of a child, it was ripped and muscular like the older members of the band, because of the long marches in the sun and rain. What was important was that the music continued for those who were grieving and those that were happy. After all, this was our bread and butter.

The next morning or afternoon after the gig, all the band members would gather in our front yard for their payments. Tatay would account and divide the payments in front of them using a sheet of paper, a ball pen, and a calculator. On the sheet, you would see a list of names of the members—Tatay and the names of the older ones would be at the top and the names of the younger ones would be at the bottom. The older members, for they played the big brass instruments, were given the larger share of the payment. We were paid based on our age and the size of our instruments. I was regarded as the youngest and the shortest so I was paid the lowest. I remember the largest sum I got was ninety pesos. This was from a fiesta where the payment was larger than what we'd normally receive in a wake. But I couldn't recall actually receiving that money. Five pesos was the largest I could ever hold. Nanay got hold of what Tatay and I earned to pay for our household's bills.

Like love, the strength of a marching band is founded on trust and respect among members. It is only on these values that you can truly say that a group or lovers really have established a relationship. Yet often, it is set aside or it disappears when doubt, envy, and ambition enter the mind and heart. As time passed by, even though I was still a child back then, I saw all of these among the band members. There were times I would witness older members divided into factions because they disagreed on issues. The younger members would often question the split in the earnings, the pieces to be performed, and the band's direction. There were times when some members would deliberately be absent from performances because of different reasons like attending something more important or if they were sick. After a few days, we found out that some of these absent members had joined the *bakyo*, the ugly and lazy band players, on the days our band would perform. Besides poaching other members, some rebels attempted to make their own marching band and became their self-appointed bandleaders.

Despite all this, I never saw Tatay furious. Although he was strict with us as his grandchildren, he was calm when talking to the band members during drinking sessions, even though he knew of their faults. I would often hear him talk about this to Nanay before they went to sleep—only thin plywood planks divided the rooms in our house—and he would also share this with some of his friends and co-teachers who'd visit and invite him to drink at home. But he didn't want to talk about it during intermissions. Even if some members attempted to talk about it, he would immediately change the topic. I witnessed all of this, perhaps because they all saw me as an innocent kid who would more likely play around and be naughty. They didn't realize that I would often stop and listen to their conversations. I was more of an eavesdropper than them.

When all these things began to happen, little by little I yearned to live with my mother and brother in Manila. My elementary graduation was nearing, and I was slowly distancing myself from the trumpet. At that time, the band would often lose contracts, and Tatay was already retired two years from teaching. This was also the time I would often see Nanay leave the house to borrow money from our relatives to pay our bills. Their old-age illnesses had also begun to appear.

Tatay decided to leave the band when my aunt married an American and petitioned both of them to live in California. I was in my first year of high school in Manila when this happened. Letters were our only form of communication. Soon, the letters were filled with complaints about the freezing weather in the country. They couldn't withstand it and in a few years, they decided to return to Candelaria. Shortly after their return, Nanay died, which eventually weakened Tatay's spirits.

Tears welcomed our family arriving at our house in Quinabuangan to hold Nanay's wake. After many years of not seeing each other, I sat beside Tatay in the front of our house. My silent, strict, and calm grandfather told a story, shaken by the memory, about his last night with Nanay in their room. How he had difficulty breathing and sleeping from the thought of not being able to take his loved one to the hospital because, just like how they started, they were the only two people left in the house. Tatay narrated this while tears gently flowed from his wrinkled face. The greying threads growing on his hair, which were once very dark and spongy, made him look older. On that day, I saw a being fade into sadness and old age in front of me. He couldn't muster the strength to play a song for his beloved even on the last night of the wake to see her off to her final resting place.

Tatay never played music again. Since Nanay's death, he always sat on a small chair outside our house in Manila and played with his grandchildren and great-grandchildren. But more often, he would stare at the greying sky. Silent. Mostly thinking. While in the province, what he was used to seeing as a lively green scenery became grey walls. Perhaps, he was always looking for the person who would express her fondness by calling him Poling. A few years later, while everyone was asleep, Tatay breathed his last from loneliness.

We returned his remains to Quinabuangan so he could be reunited with Nanay in their final resting place. The abandoned house was decorated again. Our front yard was filled with activity. Almost everyone in our barrio was in our front yard that day. They helped and chatted with our family. Some quietly paid their respects to our deceased grandfather. They hid their sadness just like us so we decided that every evening, everybody should be happy.

The D' POL PISIGAN BAND has since been disbanded. In fact, the band that played the music in Tatay's wake didn't have a name at all. But the former members—Tatay's fellow musicians who were still alive—would often visit at night but they wouldn't attempt to play anymore because of old age. In silence, I imagined them playing again beside Tatay's casket. Feelings not far from my senses. Eternal gratitude for all that Maestro Poling has taught. Melancholy for the loss of a dear friend and a mentor.

I felt shame in this sadness because, like my uncles, I never finished rehearsing the trumpet. I was also ensnared by the guitar and rock-and-roll. I did not continue our family's musical tradition—Tatay's dream, that could've been passed on to the next in line. As I left for Manila, I endlessly searched for something new for myself, never looking back to the place where I left the trumpets.

As a member of D' POL PISIGAN BAND and as my grandpa's fellow musician, I attempted to play the cymbals again in the last evening of his wake. Although I knew some of the beats, there were many other parts that I couldn't remember anymore. I quickly handed it back to the boy I had borrowed the cymbals from. I went inside the house and took Tatay's trombone that was standing beside his casket. It was rusting. The slides were broken and taped.

I stood the trombone at the centre of the band's semi-circle. And to break the silence and sadness when the band paused, I requested that they play a cha-cha. Exuberant music and dancing filled the last evening of Tatay's wake while I stared sadly at the maestro's trombone. The breath had stopped for the trombone.

It was many years later, after Tatay was buried, that I heard from a relative the painful reality of our town's musicians—they were still very poor. Because the band Tatay had given his youth and his love to organize, charged us with a fee the night they played a song for their dead band leader.

The Ship

It was a few days before I finished elementary school when we received Mama's letter from Manila. She said that I will be studying at a high school there. At that time, Mama had resigned from the sewing factory and gone back to our house in Cembo, Makati. There, she built a carinderia by a small wet market. But because her profits weren't enough to make ends meet, she asked help from Aunt Marilyn, a public school teacher, to finance my study in high school. Right away, my aunt agreed and enrolled me at the school where she taught. I was very excited because, at last, vacations weren't going to be the only reason for my visits to Manila. I was to stay there for good. I would be uprooted from the countryside.

Even though I was excited to stay in Manila and be with my mother and brother, there was sadness in my heart that I wouldn't be able to finish my training in the trumpet. One early morning in 1988 after my graduation from elementary school when I rode the bus to Manila with my grandfather, I knew I wouldn't be able to blow into the trumpet's mouthpiece again, and I wouldn't be able to see the notes on the solfege. I knew my grandfather was sad even if he never said it. His dreams of passing his music to us had been cut short. I was the last hope. From the window, as the bus passed by the town centre, I said my goodbyes to my school and the whole town but not to the memories. That day, I promised to myself that even though I never finished studying the trumpet, I would still achieve success, if not as a musician, then as somebody who went back to the home we left behind in exchange for a journey of finding our fate and discovering experiences as a high-school teenager.

After a six-hour ride, Lolo and I arrived at Guadalupe, Makati. The buildings in Manila were old; even the never-ending flux of people that came in and out of these places symbolized Manila in my mind. Add to that the smell of burning rubber from the exhaust pipes of old buses in Manila. This was the scent of Manila for me that I wanted to inhale, even though it was bad for my health. As the bus entered Epifanio Delos Santos Avenue from the north, I jutted out my neck to peer at the windows and see the Guadalupe overpass that I had been yearning to see for a long time. I remember memorizing the number of overpasses from Balintawak to Guadalupe. Because I was very excited for something I was naive about, I felt my heart beat faster in my chest.

As I alighted the bus, I immediately peed at a vacant lot underneath the 'bridge', also known as Guadalupe. I felt like a tiger peeing on the territory it wanted to possess. I did this every time I went for a vacation in Manila, but I didn't do it on purpose. My guess is it was the effect of being overly excited to arrive in Manila that the time I alighted, I felt like I had to pee. When we arrived at Cembo, I would count one by one, the moment I put the bag on the floor, the houses of my cousins, aunts, godbrothers, and godsisters. We would say our hellos, eat lunch and merienda, and of course, play. But that day at that very moment, they knew that I wouldn't just be staying there for a vacation.

My cousins gave me their old clothes to add to the very few clothes I brought along. Most were neat and beautiful clothes that they wore at home, but for me they were fine enough for outside. My other aunties promised to take care of my studies in exchange for not joining a gang. That was why the next day, from my excitement in sleeping because I was beside my mother and my brother in our old carinderia, I would part ways with them again because I had to stay at the rented house of my Aunt Marilyn in the teachers compound of a neighbouring district called West Rembo. Mama accompanied me and left me there one morning to live with my aunt who would put me to school. While watching my mother walk away from me, I promised myself that I would study very well.

Everything was new to me when classes started in 1988. From the shirt I wore to being clean and fresh. As the saying goes, from head to toe. I wore rough khaki pants, matched with a white polo shirt. There was a pocket by the left and a patch of the school logo. It said: Fort Bonifacio High School. Ironed. Finally, I could call myself a high school student. I was able to experience wearing a uniform far different from my elementary school life in the provinces where I just washed my face, changed into my clean clothes—sometimes not—and then I was ready for school. My fingernails and toenails were clean now. Auntie Marilyn sprayed cologne on me. And what I liked the most was my personal transformation because I was able to put baby oil on my hair. It gave me a wet look, and I didn't look like I had just risen from the bed. I didn't look like I was electrocuted too!

Then, of course, the school.

That day, we walked with my aunt inside a narrow pathway from her rented house and at the end of it, it said 'Ship.'

Ship was what my high school was named before it became a school; it was once a kitchen of the American soldiers when they made it a huge camp after the war. Because smoke came out of its two chimneys every time they cooked, it was called by its first inhabitants as 'like a ship'. And when it was made into a school and it experienced a very powerful storm, the Pasig river flooded there because of the unending rain and flood. The main building looked like a 'floating ship'—believe me, no joke, the structure looked like Noah's Ark! Add to this the office of the cashier that was placed beside the main building, and which coincidentally looked like the ticket booth of a pier—complete with a metal running board where new students lined up. The office had a glass window. Whoever was the architect of our school, my guess was he had a deep love for things that related to the naval industry. I guess he might have been a frustrated seaman.

But it was not in this situation that I first learnt of the 'ship'. I first knew it was called a 'cave.'

The buildings of our school back then were purely one-storeyed. If what we call the main building is the ship, there were other names for other buildings in the classrooms that divided each grade level and section. Those in First Year were to hold classes in the 'cave', which was parallel to the classrooms in front of each other and had a roofed hallway that cut through its middle. That is why if you walked, you would have felt like a train entering a dark tunnel before you reached the classroom. The other First Year sections held their classes in the 'train', which were a series of classrooms in front of the 'cave'. From what I remember, those in Grade 8 also held classes in the afternoon at the 'cave' and the 'train'. As always, the names came from the genius and creative minds of students in the school. I was pretty sure that even if the teachers denied it, even if they called the names of these buildings by their formal names in front of us, they would also sometimes use the names of these buildings in their private conversations.

I found my name at the farthest classroom at the end of the 'cave'. The list was pinned on the door. It said: Students of First Year: Section 1. The classroom was in front of a small lot where students planted vegetables for their Practical Arts subject.

The basketball gym was also beside our room. That is why on days when we were challenged to study, we would sometimes be disturbed by the noise from students planting vegetables or students playing basketball in the gym.

I felt really ashamed of myself that day. The first thing I noticed was that I was too short. My new classmates were very tall. Some were chubby. Some were tall, robust. Other girls were timid; some were grade-conscious and would right away study, and there were others who would pose alluringly and plan to become the cosmetic girl of the year. The latter would later on be known for changing boyfriends every year, be popular in dance parties, and be 'desired' as the muse of the basketball teams. So what else was there to expect? In an intense desire to know and make friends on the first day, I looked for people in the classroom who were as tall as I am. And I succeeded. I remember we were four short boys: me, Janus—who was teased and called Anus—Charlie, and Jojo.

Even on the first day, I approached Janus who was sitting at the gym during recess. My aunt had forgotten to pack my lunch, and Janus too didn't have lunch so he wanted to just sit away from the others. After I introduced myself, I said that I came from the province and told him that sometimes, I see the youth of Manila being judgmental of those from the countryside. He said that it wasn't everyone. He didn't even notice that kind of situation. The truth is, I just wanted to have somebody to talk to that day, and that's why I approached him. He was the one I saw as most approachable, and like me, shy; it was later that I found out what a naughty kid he was. From there on, Janus was one of the people I regarded as my close classmate and friend.

When I met Jojo, I remember we were only classmates in the first year, and then he was transferred to another school in the second year. There was one situation back then when a teacher told us to stand in front of the class and he asked who was cuter between Jojo and I. I didn't remember anymore why the teacher teased us that day. I didn't want to say it, but the class must be choosing an escort and the theme of the day was 'duende'. The two smallest kids in the classroom were told to stand in front of the class. The girls voted and just as I expected, I didn't win. What do I care about looking cute, when I knew that I was handsome back then!

I remember Charlie and I both liked playing video games. One day, while waiting for our Practical Arts teacher, Mr Fronda, and while some of my classmates were noisy in the Practical Arts room, both Charlie and I sat in front. Both of us short boys suddenly thought of making a scene. We made a spaceship with our seats. We acted like space rangers, completed the space missions with the sound of the spaceship *Whiiiir! Whiiiir!*, and the sound of our space guns pointed and shot at enemies—the aliens, which were our classmates—*Tsugusssh! Pukooow! Tsuguuusssh!* And because it was very noisy in the space fight, we didn't notice that 'Darth Vader' had arrived and had been watching us for a while. And that is when Charlie and I realized we were the only ones left making noise because the rest of the class at the back had suddenly gone quiet. For the whole class time, Mr Fronda punished us by making us stand on our 'spaceships' and went on to have lessons while the aliens laughed at us.

I secretly wanted to 'win' and miraculously be called cute when Jojo and I were compared to each other. I want them to know me, be popular in the classroom, and show off because I had a new crush. And it happened that I became a star in the classroom. Mrs Abril, our Visayan-speaking Maths teacher gave me my break. She didn't want anyone to enter the classroom unless they were in their proper uniform.

One day, my clothes weren't washed and I entered the classroom wearing a white t-shirt with the holy design of

Our Lord of Pardon. What was most unfortunate was that I was late by a few minutes. Mrs Abril had to abruptly stop teaching. I said my sorry. But her focus was on the clothes I was wearing. Without a word, she commanded me to remove my shirt in front of the class—in front of the short boys that I played with and the tall ones that bullied a classmate, but most of all, in front of my three crushes.

Shamefully, I slowly removed my shirt. And because I was a cry baby, a guttural sob and the flow of tears followed. My classmates stared blankly at me. I didn't know if anybody pitied me. I wasn't even done removing my shirt when I ran outside.

I learnt the concept of 'terrorism' that day before I knew the whole world today. The word Pardon, printed on my t-shirt, didn't have any power at all. But Mrs Abril was still my favourite because I knew she was serious about teaching every day. The truth is, she was the neighbour of my auntie. I wasn't able to court one of my crushes because I was shy. Who would fall in love if they saw the lanky body of the person having a crush on them and crying too! I wasn't even able to flatter them with my 'you're always on my mind.'

Because I was short in high school, I experienced bullying. Reynerio was a tall, slim guy. He had that basketball-player vibe. At first it was brought on by being 'angsty of the tall to the short', when I was suddenly teased by the fool. I answered back with a mocking tone. Because he was ashamed at being answered back by a small boy, he said I shouldn't be proud that my aunt is a teacher in the school because his mother was the guidance counsellor. Out of anger and disbelief at what he said, I shouted, 'E what? Do you want me to order your mother to pluck the grass on the fields?' Out of anger, he slapped me very hard. It was hot on the cheeks. Before we could punch each other, our cool-headed classmates went right in the middle and pulled us away from each other.

Where else were we brought but to the guidance office? And that's where I proved that Reynerio wasn't lying. Mrs Bustamante was the name on the table. Just like Reynerio's surname. I was shivering in fear. We faced his mother who was calm at first but went on to be angry when I complained about his son's bullying. In front of me, while Reynerio was pleading for his side, the mother slapped her son's lips with a ruler. Harsh. But I was glad. He deserved it, I said to myself. But when Reynerio told them that I was planning to make his mother 'pluck the grass', Mrs Bustamante looked at me for a long time and never said a word. I put my head down. I repented saying it. I wanted to fully blame Reynerio, but I knew I also had a fault. When I left school that afternoon, I cried because I was ashamed of what I had said about Mrs Bustamante. Later on, Reynerio became my friend, but not a close one. Not that quick but I became his friend right after that scene. Because of that fight, I chose to befriend those bigger than me even if I returned to the situation in elementary school where I was the sidekick of those bigger classmates who often commanded or punched me. However, my story in high school was far different.

It was in high school that I proved being tall is equal to the benefit of being seen as big.

The taller ones were drafted to play basketball and sometimes also benefitted in volleyball. It followed that some players became campus figures. They often ended up as the boyfriends of beautiful ladies in high school. And oh boy, how they changed girlfriends quarterly. Some became officials of the Citizen Advancement Training, the military training in high school. Among these, I became close to Elars and Eson, my classmates in the first section. It meant that the two weren't only big but smart too. That's why they were abundant in the benefits of being acknowledged by their teachers, classmates, and potential girlfriends. And because they were often with me, especially in the first two years of high school, they would often sprinkle me with their blessings.

I had girlfriends because my friends were popular back then. They were invited to parties of those who had crushes on them until they were invited to the houses of their future girlfriends. We would drink San Miguel Grande, one bottle each, including other classmates, using a straw at Eson's backyard beside the Pasig River. Eson would even pawn his mother's necklace just so we could experience drinking. There were times when we would stay and eat at Elar's house every Saturday. And Elars would hand me down his old shoes because mine had crumbled.

I never experienced being slaved, punched, or played by these two even though they were taller than me. We regarded each other as equals. However, I looked more like a scorer and a bodyguard while these two were flirting with their girls. There were times when they would tag me along to watch a film with their girlfriends, and as we would enter the cinema, I would act as their third wheel, watching the movie intently while the other two would be making out with their girlfriends at the topmost and darkest part of the room. I was a silent witness and sometimes, I became a voyeur, curious about what they were doing.

Later on, when we had different acquaintances and friends outside and inside the school, we remained close with each other even if the two sometimes had cold wars because of being a leader and having minions in the fields that they liked. For my part, even if my girlfriends could be counted on fingers—and no one even lasted a year—at least I graduated a virgin.

I didn't know about the two.

In my wanting to leave a mark as a student in high school, even if I was short, include my wanting to be remembered one day beside being known as 'the kid who was forced to remove his shirt while crying' back in First Year, I bravely joined the activities where I was talented. I joined the Boy Scouts and did camping. I was fond of Teodoro, the assigned leader to our group. Teod strived to do good even if he was poor like me. When we didn't have food to eat at breakfast in the camp, he introduced us to sardines with moringa leaves. And while drinking coffee and sitting in circles talking about jokes, he introduced us to a 'coffee with the cream of phlegm'. Because he laughed too hard, he sneezed so bad that the phlegm mixed with his coffee. The circle suddenly broke apart, disgusted by the sight of it.

I also used my talents in the music and arts. I played the drums in our cheering squad back in First Year—to the tune of the song 'Super Sonic'—blew the bugle in the Drum and Bugle Club, was part of the solo singing and choral competition, joint the drawing and slogan-making competitions, and contributed a poem in our school newspaper, *The Lights*. It all happened momentarily, in the four years of being a high school student. And I gained many friends because of this. High school life was fun, yes—but I proved that it was also hard for somebody like me who didn't grow up with the luxuries of life.

After my first year in high school, I went back to our old carinderia in Cembo and reunited with my mother and brother. Aunt Marilyn left the rented house. There was a fire here one early morning and many houses were burnt down. Two children died because of a gas tank explosion. Luckily, the fire lightly touched the house we were renting. That was why it was only the panties and briefs that were burnt in the comfort room. But, really the reason why I returned to my mother, was because my aunt got married and she transferred to a new house with Uncle Jess, her husband, before the fire incident. Mama didn't want me to be a burden to the new couple, and even though she was struggling herself, she strived to make me finish high school from second to the fourth year. It was hard because for a student who once had an ironed uniform now had to get used to old and stitched clothing. It was good that the Levi's 500 Jeans with the bell-bottom and button-fly became popular. Students who had money, bought the original. Those who were able to save a little, requested the seamstress to sew an imitation at the well-known Fred and Jopets in Tarikan, the upper part of the West Rembo district. Those who didn't have much but really wanted to be on the bandwagon, like me, had it 'linked' and 'triangled' by any seamstress.

I rummaged for a pair of worn pants from my uncles that were near the colour of khaki or looked for a pair of real khaki pants. If it was short, the seamstress would cut it by the knee and sew it with a cloth cut from other pants to make it longer. It was called a 'link'. The 'triangle' would happen if you wanted to make the fitted jeans into a bell-bottom. The seamstress would put a pin, cut the inseam of the pants, and sew the cut denim shaped like a triangle inside that opening. The result is a bell-bottom. Sometimes long, it was a very huge bell that somebody would annoy you by telling you were 'wearing the ears of the elephant' or you were 'sweeping the floors'. Those who were too shy would wear a bell-bottom that had an attached triangle to it. Those who wanted to be very popular had something attached—including a triangle—to almost all their pants. I was the shy one who wanted to be popular. I had three worn pants and had them altered—one with a link, another with a triangle, and the last one, with both.

Mama took turns selling food at the carinderia and washing clothes. That's why I also learnt to make ends meet. I worked as a ball boy in a tennis court inside the military camp of Fort Bonifacio during my Third Year. Mike, my younger brother, and I wouldn't have packed lunches so we often relied on the food and money given by the siblings of my mother and my grandparents. Our lives were so hard back then. There were times when we didn't have electricity at home and having a television was considered luxury.

From the First Year to Third Year, the money I spent at school was two pesos and it became three pesos when Michael and I demanded a 'raise' from Mama because I was graduating. Most of the time, my good classmates took care of me every recess. I asked for food and they shared what they had. If there weren't any 'good Samaritans' among my classmates, which was true for my Fourth Year, I had to buy food. Every Monday, Wednesdays and Friday, I would eat camote cue. It costed two pesos. I couldn't afford to buy a drink that costed P1.50 because only a peso was left from my three-peso lunch money. I would often look for a faucet where I would drink water using my hands. On Tuesdays and Thursdays, I would drink pearl-and-jelly coolers, and what was left was P1.50 that would often be spent on a pan de coco or pudding that I bought from the bakery near our house before I went to school. I secretly did it all and away from my classmates who would eat together at the canteen. I would walk away and go to a store that sold camote cue and pearl-and-jelly coolers. I didn't want to be pitied and most especially I didn't want to be teased by some ignorant classmates.

I was in Third Year when I became close to Rommel and Ogie. We joint a religious club at school called the Marian Youth Movement or MYM. Rommel was the son of my homeroom adviser and coincidentally, an adviser too of MYM, and Ogie was an honour student in class. The truth is that they were both honour students. But I wasn't one. I would normally talk to them about the lesson in class, especially about the projects. They were my serious buddies, but because I felt I had an adventurous and rebellious personality, I essentially 'belonged' to another group of friends.

Back then, when somebody said one studied at the Ship, they are known as studying in the 'most chaotic' high school in Makati. In the years I was studying there, I witnessed and became part of many brawls even if I tried not to be involved.

The school was known as a nest of warring tribes or gangs of students. These 'fraternities' had connections to popular angsty students who idled around the school and never left the memories of their life in high school. They acted like godfathers of the groups they formed. That is why every week, outside the classroom, there were no other things that the students talked about except the stories of 'which of the groups have fought, who whacked who, who was swarmed, and when did the victim fought back, who was struck by an arrow, who was hit by a sprocket, when did the goose chase happen, or where were they waiting to attack,' and many other acts of violence that gave the chaotic campus figure status to those who came out fiercer and angstier in the street brawls.

Even though I belonged to the section regarded as the cream of the crop, and was part of a religious club, I'd still look for a new adventure. I learnt to drink alcohol and smoke. I cut classes to go to the mall. As I grew older, I began to act like a gangster. I was always looking for the taste of gin and beer. I even tasted marijuana. I learnt to blame the world for the poverty my mother, brother, and I experienced, and I fought the world with a bad attitude. I answered back to the adults and always stirred up a fight. There were times when it wasn't just the notebook and ball pen that was in my bag; I also sometimes carried a cutter or a butterfly knife, and my favourite 'arrow'.

During those times, I found singing and art contests corny. I even wanted to lose my virginity to prostitutes but it never happened because I was afraid of gonorrhoea. I joined a fraternity of students inside and outside of our school, agreed to be paddled on my buttocks as a sign of my initiation, and be initiated as a fearless gang member.

That is why my mother was hurt when she found out that when I turned Fourth Year, from being a member of Section 1 for a long time, I ended up in Section 4. This was still in the category of higher sections of the school. However, because I neglected my studies in the Third Year, my high grades plummeted. When the classes started, I was ashamed of talking to my previous classmates in Section 1. I guess aside from wondering why I wasn't in my previous seat—we were in the building of the Ship—they didn't wonder about my transfer. I would often cut classes when I started working and joined a group of friends in the Third Year; there wasn't any other choice but to face my new fate and get to know my new classmates.

Knowing them wasn't hard. The first day of classes in Fourth Year, my new class adviser Mrs Sarmiento asked us about the relations of the 'senses' to people's ways of living. When the subject moved to Extra Sensory Perception or ESP, which back then was my interest because I always read about the topic in our barangay library, I was able to answer all of her questions about ESP. Up to this day, I still can't remember why on the first day of class, my adviser asked that question, and why that was the topic instead of the formal introductions of each one of us in class. It was clear that I was introduced to my new classmates with this activity. It was in this class where I fully matured as an individual that cared about others. It was different from the section where I came from because there it was always about getting the highest individual achievement, which I would see as a metric of friendships in the classroom.

In Section 4, I experienced that it was better to befriend all your classmates and join in their teasing and dreaming of studying every day. Everyone didn't have to compete for ranks and grades. It was to Noel and Randy—my first friends in that class because we sat next to each other—that I declared that I wanted to become an architect someday. They were glad because they wanted to become engineers.

I would also eat with them during recess at a bakery outside the school because the price of bread was cheaper. They would often treat me with soft drinks. They were both taller and soft-spoken. I was just talkative and short. Not later on, I also became closer to Jonathan, Eric, Allan, Jun, Mariano, Boni, Perry, and those shorter to me and very full of air, Dionisio, who we would often call OXO because he looks like a prisoner.

They would pull me away from the influence of gangs. We would be absent one day to visit an old nipa hut at the top of the mountain inside the secluded barrio of Antipolo owned by Eric's family, and here we bonded overnight with our packed canned goods, gin, rice, and guitar. We discovered that the gin wouldn't have an effect on the very cold evening weather of the mountains because not one of us brought a blanket. These simple experiences gave me the best group of friends who loved drinking and telling stories and even singing with the guitar, and not of the other group who only thought about proving their manliness and becoming popular through street brawls.

My last year of high school was the height of the age of rock bands. Bon Jovi, Extreme, Mr Big, and many others. Those who wanted a showstopper with the guitar should know how to strum a song from one of these bands. Eric and I were obsessed with songs from Asin, folk songs by Simon and Garfunkel to 'Living on a prayer' by Bon Jovi and 'More than Words' by the Extreme. Our classmate Bermejo, who we would often call 'Ernie Barong' because he mimicked the voice and the mannerisms of the famous weatherman, was the one who would always share stories about watching 'guitar competitions' and excitedly imitate them. The fool liked metal bands. The band Megadeth was his favourite and would later on be a significant influence in his life as a musician. I never saw him play the guitar in high school but after many years, in a gig where our college bands performed, Bermejo was the fastest strummer on the guitar. He became a 'monster' rockstar who inspired many others in Makati who wanted to learn to play the guitar.

Our time was also the time of man-made and nature-made disturbances and calamities like today. We witnessed the scheduled brownouts. Sometimes we would call Ms Borja before and she would ask, 'Jarin! [in her infamous loud voice], what is the concept of Economic Demand?!' Ha! Of course, I didn't know the answer. I just came from cutting classes in the morning with some of my classmates in Section 1 and I felt the beer kicking in. I was shaking when I stood up and prepared myself to be laughed at because I didn't know the answer, when suddenly a strong earthquake happened! I saw the underwear of my two batch mates who immediately ducked in the corridor while the flagpole swung like a compass. It was 16 July 1990. I was saved from a huge embarrassment thanks to the earthquake. We also didn't experience the Junior Senior Prom, because there was always violence, and even deaths, at the Ship. Some would get pregnant at every JS Prom. Later on, we couldn't forget when the Ship burnt. I wasn't sure if this was before or a few days after our graduation. We ran to the high school and couldn't believe what was once our place of boyhood and girlhood was consumed by flames. There was angry screaming; some cried especially the girls. And because the students of the Ship were 'geniuses and creative', some guys gambled on which room would burn first. There was clapping and cheers for whoever got the correct guess.

I left the province to be a young man by becoming the Ship's passenger. From the hardships of life, socializing and introducing one's mark, I had success in gaining new friends and deeper wisdoms of life brought by my experiences.

Sailing with the Ship ended on my graduation day in 1992. That day, I admired our Valedictorian bowing by wearing many medals. But after that, I went home to our small carinderia and removed my toga while Mama was calling us to eat dinner. And before I slept, I prayed that I would have many medals and successes someday. Outside the Ship. To enter it again.

After nineteen years, I was invited as a guest speaker on the Recognition Day of my former school, as a teacher who now taught the concept of Economic Demand that I was never able to answer before the earthquake. I noticed the school's Ship didn't look familiar anymore. There was cement in its place. No more wood. No more rooms that look like caves and trains. No more trees and thick covers where lovers could hide or classmates could drink and smoke, and those macho frat boys striking neophytes with paddles. I learnt that the students were then called Bonifacians and the Ship's name was changed to Super Ferry. The buildings had become taller like a modern ship. I laughed very hard at the sight of it all.

Ball Boy

There are times while riding my motorcycle that I intentionally pass by a place that contributed to shaping who I am today. At times like this, I wasn't going home nor was I going to an exact place. I just really want to pass by the old places I used to walk through. The wind would blow into my hard helmet, bringing with it memories that I experienced—the sadness, joy, fear, questioning, and astonishment in places I return to or that I will go through again.

This place has transformed itself. What were once huge tracts of grassland and forest are replaced by high-rise buildings, malls, and restaurants. What used to be the exclusive dwellings of only one sector of society are now commercialized subdivisions. Add to this the names of new wide roads that have been narrowed or obstructed since the past decade. Even though I often get lost in its current state as a concrete forest of the affluent and no longer a real forest that everyone passed through, I still come back to this place, now better known as The Fort.

Before the Bonifacio Global City in Taguig came to be known as The Fort, we knew it as Fort Bonifacio, a military camp. One of the districts there is Cembo, which was our village, near the camp. And it was not covered by Taguig then. Fort Bonifacio is known as part of Makati. Those from Cembo and neighboring villages who want to enter the military, whatever its branch, have focused their dreams inside Fort Bonifacio. The day will come when they will be among those who will train there and become soldiers of the country. Even those who want to get rich as seafarers also dream of getting into it. Also, inside it was the old Philippine Merchant Marine Academy (PMMA) where many of my classmates who did not want to become soldiers dreamt that one day, after high school, they would pass as PMMA cadets.

Many soldiers also live in the surrounding villages, including ours, especially those who already have a family. Although more civilians began living in the villages surrounding the camp by the 1980s, the military culture was still felt here. It is common to see green owner-type jeeps with the tag 'For Official Use Only' move in and around the villages. Even when I was in high school towards the early 1990s, almost all who served as captains and village councillors were previously in the service. That is why even though Makati is the city attached to our barangay, the official address we always wrote was Cembo, Fort Bonifacio, Makati. Fort Bonifacio must be attached to its name. It is a manifestation that the barangays belonging to the Second District of Makati City have been discovered, enriched, and upheld by soldiers since time immemorial during and after the Second World War because they were said to be just fields of grass and mudflats before they were transformed and turned into a village.

I am not one of the descendants of the soldiers. Even though my father was a soldier in the army, he was also from the far-flung province of Imus, Cavite and only settled in Cembo because of my mother. They also met inside the camp. My mother was guarding her aunt's shop when my father courted her. It didn't last long because they also got separated. I was born in the camp's Philippine Army Hospital, but didn't grow up in Cembo. Because of my parents' separation, my brother Mike and I went to Quinabuangan.

I returned to Cembo when I was high school; I would live with my mother and brother again in an old carinderia that also became our makeshift home in the middle of what was once a small wet market in Cembo. Here in this carinderia, we would sometimes experience skipping meals. Sometimes my mother was too broke to buy ingredients to sell at least four pots of cooked food. Time passed by and the opportunity for her to sell food seemed like a meteor away, so she finally closed the store. We relied on the help of relatives and when that wasn't enough, we came to a point where we would be cut off from electricity. Later on, Mama sold our pet dog for 300 pesos to the drunkards on our streets so we could pay our bills. Sometimes to curb our hunger, we would divide a half kilo of sweet potatoes to last for a day. Because of the curse of the sweet potato, Mike and I would often hide behind our village's tall grasses to poop because we didn't even have the luxury of a toilet.

These situations that I experienced in high school also made me dream of getting inside Fort Bonifacio. But I didn't want to join the army or be a cadet. I couldn't wait for that anymore. I needed something that could make easy money back then. I wanted to enter that place even though I was young to work at the golf course or tennis court of the military officers in the camp. I was just in my first year of high school when I heard the news that the courts were hiring for this great part-time job. Rumour has it that military officers, especially the ladies—what they called the officers' wives—gave large tips to ball pickers whenever they played golf or tennis.

I had the courage to make this 'immediate dream' happen one day, after I heard from Mama that Mike made money by forcing himself to throw away many plastic bags of accumulated 'excrement' from our Japanese neighbour who also didn't have a toilet. I challenged myself to earn and help Mama as well. Desperate times come with desperate measures—as for Mike, he toughened his stomach.

But I didn't throw poop like Mike did. I 'picked up' balls. I became the 'ball boy' of the tennis court.

I had a classmate in Third Year who was a transferee at Fort Bonifacio High School. From what I remember, his name was Reynaldo Bayang. We called him 'Bayang.' I befriended him and became very close so I chose not to associate with those who teased him and secretly called him without the letter 'n' from 'Bayang'—'balls' in English. What I remember most about him is the big and lively mole on his face. But he became a significant part of my life when I found out he lived at the Joint United States Military Advisory Group (JUSMAG), an exclusive officers' village within the camp. He was a close relative or adopted son of a retired military officer. And most importantly, he had a connection to the area's tennis court. I did not miss this precious chance so I asked him to help me get in as a ball picker in the camp's tennis court. I said I could do it from afternoon to evening each day after my classes. One day, he accompanied me to talk to Brother Robert, the manager of the tennis court and the ball boys.

Even before I met him, the students of our school, including me, went to JUSMAG because it had a swimming pool that was rented for fifteen pesos. I also rented used swimming trunks for rent for ten pesos. You could pretend to be a rich kid by swimming for twenty-five pesos, along with your classmates who also pretended to be rich in this hygienic swimming pool, while you prayed that the first person who wore your rented trunks didn't have ringworms.

But getting back to our story—it was Bayang who introduced me to Kuya Robert. He was young and had a huge physique but he didn't have that bully vibe. He can even pass as an executive at Ayala if he dresses up in business fashion. Brother Robert looked at me from head to toe. He shook his head. He said I was too small—eh, I was actually one of the smallest in my class back then. I might get tired from picking up the ball right away. I was afraid of not being accepted so what could I do but sell myself. I told him that I ran very fast—this is true because I was a track and field runner and a patintero player in elementary school—and I was also good at picking up balls. This is also true because I was a ball picker on the other side of the school fence in elementary school. Because I was short, I was the only one who could get through the gap under the wire fence, and I was the only one picked on by my taller classmates.

Kuya Robert was quickly impressed and agreed right away. I went right ahead, adding the recommendation of my 'manager' Bayang. In Third Year high school, I had my first job for my family. Part-time, yes, but still work. Ferdie, the ball boy, already made money. How much? Ten pesos a game. It was already big for someone like me with only two pesos for a school allowance. The food was so delicious because I bought it from hard work and play. But my mission was to taste real home-cooked food, even meals simply cooked with meat. Or lots of toasted galunggong or fried vegetables with anchovies or small dried shrimps. Just simple dishes. I never dreamt of eating beef stroganoff back then, a dish that I would have whenever there was an occasion. I just wanted to get rid of our sweet potato diet and its farting side effects.

When I got in, I was the twelfth of the ball boys. The 'competition' was fierce. We also offered ourselves every time we saw a car coming and the officers, ladies, and other able-bodied people came over to play tennis. We would race and the first one to meet them would open their car door or carry their belongings into the tennis court. And there were times we would also wipe their rackets or invite them to buy soft drinks before playing. Some of us even resorted to massaging their foreheads for free as well as washing their car tires. In other words, we were no different from errand boys. We would do everything to catch their attention so when they played, they would point out the 'most industrious', the 'most accommodating', and the 'most obedient' boy as the lucky ones who would pick up their very fragrant, greener than green, and semi-flaccid tennis balls.

If you set aside the technical terms, it's really simple to play tennis. The player will only ensure that the served ball will fall on the other side of the net where the opponent is. And the opponent is positioned un-parallel to him. Because if the ball falls on the side opposite the one who served, the umpire, the game's guide, will shout 'Fault!' The score goes to the opponent. Some players only wanted 1–15 points. Some seem to want to live on the tennis court because their desired score was 1–21. This is just the first round. The score was repeated in the second round. And if you were unlucky—for all of us ball boys, it was too tiring to run and pick up the balls add to this that we are also scoring—each rival won with one round, there would be a third round or the so-called decision round. As long as you kept hitting the ball back to the opponent and the ball fell within the limits of the court, the opponent won't be able to score on you.

As a ball boy, apart from the fact that you must run fast to pick up the ball that was not caught by the player's blow, you must also be able to return the ball to anyone who serves with just one bounce. No matter how far away you are from the serving position, you can't come near him. With a bounce, he should have caught the ball in his hand.

Of course, at first, I made a lot of mistakes here. Many times, the old ball boys laughed at me. There was one time when I returned the ball by approaching the serve. Or I won't return it because I thought I still had a spare ball in my pocket to serve. Sometimes the player would scold me because I didn't score and enjoyed watching the game. There was really no formal training to be a ball boy. If you don't ask the older ball boys—some are impatient to answer—you won't know how to play the game. After all, the day Brother Robert accepted me, he just said: 'Oh, observe them first, you'll join later.' It was only about thirty minutes, then I became a ball boy without really knowing what to do. Later, when I became close to him, I asked him and found out that it was his style to all beginners. A trial by fire. Learning from one's mistakes. Well, it worked for me.

The time came when I had patrons and no matter what else my teammates did, I was really the one they wanted to pick up their balls even if they waited for me to finish picking up the ball from another player. There were many reasons. There were players I bought soft drinks for over and over without me complaining, even though I had to repeatedly run to a distant store and back to the court. The late actress Nida Blanca once played there. I was her ball boy. She was beautiful even at an old age. It was to her that I was first star struck! She even gave me a twenty-peso tip because she said I was fast.

There was a time when with the excessive force and height of a soldier's stroke, the ball got stuck between the steel ceiling of the gym. The ball was too high. Who else would get it? I nervously climbed to get the ball. There was no problem climbing because I did it right away. The problem was the crossing of the irons towards the ball. It was far from where I was after the climb. Honestly, my whole body was shaking because they didn't even ask me if I was afraid of heights. If they just asked me, I would answer with 'Yes! Yes! Yes! Yes! Really! Swear! No joke! Really-really-really!' And since I wasn't asked, I climbed up and crossed the irons secretly praying that I wouldn't be tempted to look down. I really stared at the damn fucking ball. And I successfully got it down while the players clapped. I felt good afterwards. Aside from becoming very handsome in their eyes—even the soldier who hit the ball on the ceiling promised that if I wanted to join the Air Force someday, he would recommend me—I also overcame my fear of heights. I felt like a winner that day! So from then on, when they were there to play, they would tell Brother Robert that the boy they wanted to pick up the ball was the 'hardworking kid' or the 'kind one'.

I also used to have fun when I wasn't ball-picking and when I became close to some of the players; I would talk to them, especially the older ladies who also loved telling stories. I was interested to know about their lives. They often said that they have children my age who are studying abroad. I secretly got jealous when I heard this. I also secretly dreamt that they would adopt me so that I could raise my mother and brother from poverty. Even if I didn't have to study abroad. Perhaps just own many pairs of school uniforms, a slick notebook, and lots of ball pens. And most of all, I would always have a packed lunch. A delicious one and share mine with a classmate who didn't have food. But of course, they didn't do that. Even if they were kind to me. Only babies are adopted. And a cute baby for that matter. Not a cute boy! The suburban matron ladies feared of being gossiped about 'cradle snatching' if they ever adopted me. I eventually abandoned that delusion.

Having customers means also having jealous rivals. I had this among my fellow ball boys. At that time when I was working as a ball boy, three of them were not happy with what I was doing. They complained that I liked to snatch clients. He said I could refuse even if I wanted to so that they could also make money. And they even said I kept talking to clients just to get patrons. If I was afraid of heights, I wasn't afraid of fighting even if they were three. Even though they were bigger than me. Make me hungry but don't accuse me of anything.

I told them that my conversation was not about showing off but an initiative and being quick and diligent was my way of showing effort. I also said that if they chose to get acquainted with the clients, they should do so as ball pickers rather than sleeping away. That way, they wouldn't lose a client. After that I challenged them to a fist fight outside the court. One by one. I said I wouldn't stop them. It didn't work out because Brother Robert intervened and scolded us all.

I didn't know if they understood the word initiative and effort. Not to humiliate people, but many of the ball boys I worked with back then were not students. In fact, from what I remember, I was the only student among them. Most of them came from the provinces of Visayas and Mindanao. They had large physiques and hard muscles that obviously got ripped from working in the province—I was just brave but if the quarrel continued, I was sure these three would find their place. Some of them dreamt of joining the army so they went to Fort Bonifacio. Lacking in height, failing the battery exam, they were sent to JUSMAG to pick up balls because they did not want to return to their families in the province hoping that they would be soldiers here in Manila. They were very old compared to me. Some were really dirt poor just like me so it was hard to be there.

Pol and I, the Tagalogs, were the only ones from Makati. So we often talked with each other. We were also close in age but he wasn't a student. Orphaned and living with his aunt, Pol had to pick up balls to help his aunt's large family if he didn't want to get evicted from her house. Sometimes, when he knows he has little income, he won't go home to his aunt and just sleep with our colleagues who live behind the tennis court. Many of the provincial ball boys had already built small dwellings here, attached to those of Brother Robert's house, from the proceeds of lumber, galvanized iron, plywood and others found in some abandoned and dilapidated military houses in the vicinity. It was well made just that, because there were so many of them, they're like sardines inside these makeshift houses. This is where Pol squeezed himself in.

Every Saturday and Sunday, I worked all day. Every time we rested and ate, Pol and I didn't part. We often shared that spicy red Young's Town Sardines. We would often pitch in to buy it. Then, we would also contribute to our colleagues to buy rice. As soon as we opened the sardines and added a little lime and soy sauce to them, we immediately poured them over the steaming rice. It didn't matter if your finger and tongue were still burning. In less than five minutes, the sardines and rice will be swimming in our stomachs. And we would sip iced water from plastic containers until we burped.

We were content with this kind of life. We would later on take a bath outside the tennis court on a vacant lot. We took turns holding the water hose so that one could bathe. I just soaped myself because I saw Pol had lots of white spots from his face to his chest and back. He looked like a dalmatian. I doubt the madman had a jock itch. I would sometimes catch him scratching his groin while picking balls. That's why I also ate from my own plate. It was hard to share with Pol. We often shook hands, but I don't want to rub my nose if there were fungi on his hands. Still, Pol is my friend. That's what matters even if I never told him the real reason why I had my own soap and plate.

When I was in Third Year high school, my classes ended at twelve o'clock in the afternoon. I'll go home and have lunch of whatever Mama cooked that day. Then, I would quickly change my clothes and board the Guadalupe-Gate 3 jeepney, which was the only means of transportation for the homeless inside Fort Bonifacio. I was still witness to the 75-cent fare back then. In about ten minutes, I was at JUSMAG and ready to pick up the balls. From Monday to Friday, I earned a lot of money from

picking balls up to six games. That's sixty pesos. I didn't have
to extend beyond five o'clock in the afternoon. I still have to do
my homework. On Saturdays and Sundays, I picked balls from
the morning until seven in the evening. Since all the ball boys
were there, in those days the competition was fierce. I relied on
patrons and you prayed they would think of playing that day.
The biggest income I brought home was 100 pesos. We would
have a feast at home. Tocino and longganisa were served on
the table. Noodles or fried vegetables accompanied these. There
will be more breakfast the next day. I often saved five pesos, my
daily allowance, for my income. When I wasn't picking balls,
Mama could only give me two pesos for my lunch money while
my classmates were already bringing 10 or 20 pesos. For an
increase of five pesos, I was able to keep up with my classmates
who bought sodas and bread in the canteen during recess.
I didn't have to hide and feel shamed in a distant store and buy
sweet potato cue and jelly coolers every day when I only had
two pesos. Somehow, when I became a ball boy, my first job, my
family and I felt a little comfortable in our small residence, the
carinderia that never sold food.

One day, I liked Jose Marie Chan's song, the 'Beautiful Girl.'
Then, it was followed by another popular hit, 'Constant Change.'
There was no CD player, iPod, or MP3 back then. Cassette
tapes were still the star. And Chan's album was 75 pesos. I made
it an 'attainable dream' to buy his album. I saved money from
my income as a ball boy. Two weeks passed by before I raised
the money to buy the tape. And one rainy Saturday morning,
I asked permission from Brother Robert who came to work in
the afternoon, and told him I had something important to buy
for class. Of course this was not true. I was already imagining
Chan's face on the album that would soon be mine in a few
moments. When he agreed, I hurriedly took a jeepney to Ayala,
entered a well-known mall and was on my way to the second

floor where the music store was located when beautiful clothes on sale suddenly appeared on the first floor. And then, the fragrance of the burger wafted from a fast food restaurant.

I had a hard time deciding on things that day. Although I dreamt of being flattered by Chan's romanticism and bourgeois songs because of the beauty of the melodies he created, I also dreamt of buying myself a shirt and tasting a delicious hamburger. Not fish, noodles or fried vegetables but hamburgers. And it was hard for Chan to flatter while I had on my mind the soft, clean, and cheap clothes as well as the fragrant hamburger. So I didn't reach the 'attainable dream'. I dressed myself in clothes for 40 pesos each and ate hamburgers, fries and soft drinks for 25 pesos. I still had 10 pesos left! And so I was excited to go home after dinner. I immediately put on the white shirt with Goofy's big face on the front. Goofy's tongue is prominent in the design so I liked it. I love to show Mama and Mike what I 'bought' with my hard-earned money when I remembered that I still had to go back as a ball boy in the afternoon.

It was still raining when I got back to JUSMAG. Hardly anyone was playing except those in the gym because there was a roof on it. I went straight to Brother Robert's little house to let him know that I had arrived. But I did not talk to him. I saw that he was sound asleep. When I moved to the residences of my fellow ball boys, many were also asleep. They had just finished eating lunch and because it was raining, it was siesta time. I saw Pol huddled in a corner sleeping. I don't know why on that day, I wanted to stare at his face for a long time. I left quietly, did not say goodbye, and went home. As might be expected, my mother was pleased with the shirt. Mike wanted me to buy him a shirt too. I promised I would save money for his new shirt and that he could borrow my Goofy tee for a while. Mike wore my Goofy shirt for a long time but I was never able to keep my promise to him.

I haven't returned to JUSMAG since that day. I never said a word of goodbye to Brother Robert, Pol and the other ball boys. Many more days will pass before I could ask Bayang to tell Brother Robert and my former co-workers that I was very grateful for the opportunity and experience to work as a ball boy. I didn't last a year in that work. Before classes ended, tons of schoolwork stopped me from picking balls. I would also join a gang and find myself afraid of losing my youth to the toils of working. I learnt a lot of bad habits. I tried to love. I felt the pain and heaviness of young love and some failed expectations. And that's when I finally realized I couldn't pick up the balls anymore.

Two decades later, Fort Bonifacio has become very different. All the surrounding villages, including ours, no longer have 'Fort Bonifacio' attached to the address. We are solid residents of Makati City—even though the court has currently ruled that we are covered by Taguig. It is a manifestation that the era of this military village is over. You will no longer see green owner-type-jeeps with 'For Official Use Only' signs roaming within the villages. The former military camp is now a commercialized area. Everywhere you look, buildings for businesses stood: restaurants, malls, condominiums, car shops, BPOs, function venues and many others have erased and buried the former golf courses and tennis courts of the camp, as well as their former exclusive residences. Even their military museums were not forgiven. In fact, in Cembo we heard gunshots from the military men fighting to save their homes from government demolition teams and businessmen. Most of them were enlisted personnel and junior officers because senior military officers quickly devised a way to create an exclusive subdivision for them away from the boundaries of the commercialized area before it was even built. In my view, after the 'Coup Era' of Gringo Honasan and his boys of the Reform the Armed Forces Movement, new tensions were born among old and young officers and soldiers in the military, which erupted in the uprising of the Magdalo faction in the present. This tension continues to be felt even if they hide it completely.

Proof of this is also what happened and continues to happen in JUSMAG. Current military officers, just a few years ago, expelled their former retired generals. They are justified in allowing those who are still in service to live in the area. And it is said to be a place not for retirees who only stay there because of political influence. The problem will be even bigger because at present, it is claimed by the commercial interests that will be connected to The Fort. Coincidentally, no soldier will benefit from JUSMAG even if it is loyal to their grandstand. They are also victims of land conversion by the government they protected and of capitalism by the businessmen-politicians they considered executive officers.

With news like this, I looked back on the memory of being a ball boy at JUSMAG. I also wondered what has happened to my colleagues and acquaintances there and what has become of their lives since I left them. I can no longer remember their names and faces. Did Pol get married and have a child? Is Brother Robert still there or has he started his own family? Are my patron soldiers and matron ladies still alive? Did they become allies in so many tensions and issues within their organization that playing tennis could not be solved? Is the tennis court still there? Could it be that some of my former associates still continue to pick up the ball despite getting older and having a family? Or were Pol, Brother Robert, and the other ball boys still victims of poverty caused by commercial greed in the area? Commerce has never valued its workers. These are unanswered questions because I never saw these people again. These places are now covered with towering buildings and wider roads. Noise from rushing private cars has become more deafening to even hear the answers from the bouncing of the tennis ball.

On some occasions, I pass by the places that I know have contributed to shaping my character. I don't just simply pass by. The truth is, I pick up memories of experienced sadness, joy, anxiety, questioning, or astonishment. I know these experiences shaped who I am today. And with how often I travel like this, and with the amount of memories I want to go back to and cherish, I'm very sure, on the inside, I'll stay a ball boy forever.

Niog

When we were kids, my brother and I would be teased by our aunts and uncles that we're not really from Candelaria or Cembo. We were actually from Cavite, specifically the town of Imus because our father was said to be from there. This happened when they asked jokingly if we knew our dad. I was only three years old and Mike was a year old when my father left us. We only had a vague memory of his face.

Since childhood, even though I have never been to any town in Cavite, I felt annoyed and angry on hearing the name of that place. I even said before that I will never set foot in Cavite even when I am old. But as life continued to change, these feelings also disappeared. Experience will really tell what photos we want to put in the album of each other's lives. Even our most avoided place.

During the summer vacation before my second year of high school, I had an adventure in Cavite when my Uncle Ciel took me to help in his little shop. I needed money to buy stuff for the next school year. All this would happen in the far-flung district called Niog, with the help of Uncle Ciel and Aunt Zeny.

My uncle was a messenger who settled in Cavite when he met Aunt Zeny who was then a saleslady at Anson's, an appliance store in Makati. When Uncle Ciel bought furniture from the store, he also sold his heart to Aunt Zeny and they were both swept by this whirlwind romance, and they eventually lived in Barangay Niog in Bacoor Town. Since then, my uncle's story has always compared the appearance of his new residence, which he said was very different from Cembo. Even the people's accents and customs were very different. In fact, there were times when I noticed the strangeness of his accent when speaking. It was evident that he was becoming more Caviteño than Manileño. When I heard it over and over in his stories, little by little these stories completely erased the image of Cavite on my mind that I have likened to the image of my father. I imagined new adventures in new places that I wanted to reach. I was excited about new experiences outside of Cembo. Or maybe I still missed life in the countryside because I had fond and deep memories there. So one day when Uncle Ciel visited Cembo again, I asked him to take me to Bacoor.

Barangay Niog is divided in two. The Niog I went to was on the right side of Aguinaldo Highway so it was called Niog Dos while Niog Uno was on the left side. And the barangay hall itself is the opening of the town of Bacoor, which is the opening town of the province of Cavite if you come from Baclaran. My uncle's in-laws' house is just steps away from the very centre of Niog. One of the shops lined up on this street is Uncle Ciel's sari-sari store. All the houses lined up on the side of the street are what they called labasan and of course, the looban—large houses that are quite a distance away from the streets and those behind the labasan households. Big houses are in the labasan and small houses are in the looban. It is also strange to think that if you are standing on the street, the right side of the looban has houses that are no different from the looks of the houses of the often called informal settlers in Manila while the left side of the looban are hut-like houses in the province. Most of the population is found in the looban and will go out to the labasan when they need to buy at my uncle's store, which is well positioned on the very street where the locals from the looban exit. It was very different from the circular structure of the community that I grew up with in Cembo. And here, almost everyone knows each other. The crowds are thicker and more scattered.

I helped Aunt Zeny with shopping, sales and other household chores while spending my vacation in Niog. Sometimes I babysat their children, Earl and Irish. I almost resembled their children because they inherited the looks more from Uncle Ciel so I was sometimes mistaken for the couple's eldest son by assuming and gossiping customers of the store. Auntie Zenyang was the simplest and kindest mother I have ever known because she didn't know how to be angry and she was always smiling. Because Uncle Ciel was often late at night when he came home from work, Aunt Zeny acted as my guide there. Eventually, Aunt Zeny considered me her son. She also jokingly introduced me as her 'firstborn' to customers who asked who the new store-keeper was. At first, I was confused about the prices and where exactly the containers were placed. But I eventually learnt the tools of the trade, and the time came when Aunt Zeny entrusted me to sell and manage the store during the day. I would also travel to the neighbouring town of Bacoor like Binakayan because she would order me to buy our bread supply from there.

Whenever I was at the store selling goods, I quickly set aside the profits, made an inventory of the sold goods, especially weighing kilos of rice bought by customers. It was a bit boring when one bought little amounts of lard, soy sauce, and vinegar. It slowed down the action because I had to properly open the opaque plastic containers and gently measure them until I transferred them to the plastics using a small funnel. There was no problem if one bought only a few items. But often, because many people were simultaneously buying, I would curse those who bought little sachets of ingredients. So it was common that my shirt would get splashed with these liquids, especially in the afternoon when people were rushing to cook dinner and will join in buying those who also bought rice. At times like this, I asked for the help of any of the siblings, either Joey, Annie, or Venus who were Aunt Zeny's nephew and nieces. These siblings were my first friends in Niog because they also lived in the house of my uncle's in-laws. They never hesitated to help.

I would become close to them as well as to Aunt Zeny's mother, Mother Linda, who was very active in the church. There were times when Mother Linda took me to processions of the saints as well as to the rosary praying. She also often introduced me as her grandchild at these gatherings. Aunt Zeny's father was a barber in Niog. Yet, unlike the other barbers who liked telling stories, her father was the one I haven't even talked to for a long time. He was a very quiet person, especially at home. You could only hear him speak when he was doing haircuts inside his barbershop stationed at the back of the store.

Among the siblings, I first got close to Annie. She was my age, a pretty girl with a dark complexion and an Indian-like beauty. She often accompanied me to the shop. We also often talked about lessons at school. It came to a point that we wanted to see each other every day. Even as children, we knew we felt differently every time we were together. But we knew we couldn't fall in love, especially me. I could only imagine stealing a kiss from Annie, even though I know she wouldn't avoid it. But I could already see in my mind the angry faces of Uncle Ciel, Aunt Zeny, and Mother Linda. I might be sent home to Cembo in no time. So I immediately abandoned the idea. I simply avoided Annie. She wasn't angry because at that time she had many girls who became her besties. What makes this beautiful for young people of this age who 'feel something' is that it is easy to forget because they are quickly preoccupied with new experiences and choices. It is also because new acquaintances and friends kept coming—in Niog they called them their 'troops'. And at that time, I had a lot of squads, buddies with whom I learnt to smoke.

One day, Joey whom we called Joy, the eldest son of the siblings, came into the room next to the store. He begged me not to tell that he was a smoker. He snatched a stick of More from his pocket and lit it. Since there were only two of us in the room that day, and there weren't many buyers at noon, the fool was brave enough to blow smoke rings. As I watched him, I also felt the urge to try what he was doing. And the fool also felt it. He suddenly grabbed me with a stick and started our 'smoking tutorial'. My cough got worse when he said that I should inhale the smoke before I exhaled. He said that it is wrong for me to exhale it immediately after inhaling. I should not blow like a 'dragon.' And because his 'student' was a fast learner, the afternoons that followed became my regular smoking sessions with Joy. However, I got dizzy. He said it was always like that at first. I would prove that this is true because by the second week, the dizziness would be gone and it would be replaced by the taste of nicotine and the sweetness of blowing smoke rings from the cigarette. And when Joy felt that I was ready, one night he took me to their troop to teach me how to drink and get to know Gary, Nora, Deo, Benjie, Bani, and many others. They would be my troops in Niog.

Eventually, I graduated from More and was blown away by the promising Champion Blue that is the preferred cigarette of the men of Niog. At the same time, I always asked permission from Aunt Zeny every night to hang out with Joy and come back home drunk. And like Uncle Ciel who had many friends in Niog because he serenaded the drinkers with his guitar, becoming close to my new Caviteño troops was not be any different here. I was the guitarist and the singer of my troop. The rest was my back-up. They also bought the drinks and the snacks. Nora—named after the big mole on her face like the famous Filipina dark-skinned actress Nora Aunor—often acted as our storyteller during our drinks. I would imitate how they dress as well. In Binakayan, I bought thick belts with wide buckles, and a white Hanes shirt that will be tucked into jeans with a double hem. I would wear a wide scarf that intentionally dangled from the back of the jeans pocket. I also used a Suave balm on my 'kempee' hair—the parting of the hair was in the middle and it looked like a cow had licked it with shine. The glowing Champion Blue would be stuck between the fingers. That is how we all looked at parties that we went to in the nearby villages. And in order for me to be a full-fledged Caviteño, I spoke with their accents and called everyone not by name but by saying 'Boy!' Because I already belong to a troop and I felt like a young man from Niog, I believed that one day I'll have the courage to meet a girl.

There was a child who used to talk to me when I was buying soft drinks. His name was Erwin. That child was so talkative. He was so animated when he told stories, especially about new games. Their house was parallel to the store and if I looked to the left, I could see it immediately. Sometimes he would tell me stories about his beautiful sister, Evelyn. He said we were a match. So I told him, then why won't he introduce me to his sister. Of course, I was just kidding. I took his story as a joke. But he took it seriously. One afternoon, he pretended to ask his sister to buy him something from the store. He insisted on bringing her to the store. And I have proven that children do not lie. Especially when I saw the mole on Evelyn's chin, it looked even more beautiful in my eyes. As I handed Erwin the chips they bought, Evelyn was embarrassed to look at me.

From then on, the kid would frequently ask his sister to accompany him in buying from the store until it came to a point when Evelyn would intentionally buy from our store on her own. I took this chance and formally introduced myself to her. Erwin would be our middle man in sending letters written on a fragrant paper. One day, Erwin called me because his sister wanted to meet me in the basement of their house. I would quickly go downstairs and there, Evelyn would become my girlfriend and allow me to kiss her cheeks. I have never felt happier than that day. Soon, I would not hang out anymore with the troops because I preferred to talk to Evelyn. In these conversations, I will learn that their mother worked in Hong Kong and she had an older sister and brother. I also told her stories about my life in Cembo. It was like this every night. It was full of love that my young heart felt back then. And there was nothing more serious to me then than the relationship I found in Niog.

Evelyn gave a different colour to my life at Niog. So when the holidays were over, my young heart was crushed as Uncle Ciel and I walked down Niog Street to travel back to Manila. As we passed in front of Evelyn's window, I could see her eyes sadly following me as I walked away. Cellphones weren't fashionable back then for texting so on a few weekends when I saved up for a fare, I dared myself to travel alone to Niog just to see her. Days passed by and she rarely came out of the house to meet me even though I had traveled from far away. She wanted to focus on studying. She also told me that her sister scolded her because we were still too young to fall in love. Eventually, I lost the drive to go back to Niog because I got busy studying. Despite the pain I experienced from the demise of our relationship, I would return as a storekeeper by the next vacation and get to know two people who would become closer to my heart.

I met Inying. He was the garbage collector of many sari-sari stores in Niog. Inying was old. He would be considered a grandpa if he had grandchildren. His skin was burnt and the clothes he wore were always so dirty that I only see them being changed once. According to lore, one day he suddenly appeared out of nowhere in Niog and offered himself to be the garbage collector of the stores. This was a big help to the vendors so Inying was easily able to adapt in the barangay. However, Inying often drank. Because instead of paying five pesos for his disposal, he would just ask the store owners to pay him a bottle of Tanduay rum. Whenever this drunkard tried to play with children on the streets, the children would often run away from him and tease him, 'Inying is going crazy again!' When Inying visited our store, he wouldn't ask to hand over the garbage. He would first request to pass him a bottle of rum and would often stop for a quick chat before leaving. He would tell lots of stories because I also like asking questions about his life.

I found out that he is from a province in the Visayas. He didn't have a family anymore and worked in almost all the heaviest and dirtiest blue-collar jobs you could think of in Manila. He never told me why he no longer had a family. It's just that every time I asked him about it, he would suddenly shut up and his eyes would get sad. His silence and sadness was noticeable because he was naturally talkative and cheerful especially when drunk. I would even laugh at his voice when it suddenly became like a stuttering kid because his upper teeth were missing. He often ended our conversation with a Visayan song number that, of course, I couldn't understand because he was out of tune. But he always called me 'with a friend' and it was at this moment I realized that I really liked to make friends, especially to those I felt have been wronged by others.

Just like Ali.

Once when I was babysitting Irish, Aunt Zeny's youngest child, I made her sit on the window sill of the house because I got tired carrying her. Moments later, I heard shouting from outside the house. I looked out the window and there I saw Ali first. He was carrying his young brother in his arms, fighting with an aunt who wanted to evict them from the land where their little house stood. I could clearly see the tension on Ali's face while defending his right to stay on the lot, answering back to the endless reprimands of his aunt. They didn't know I was witnessing everything from the window.

Ali was not wearing nice clothes, not even his brother. I would later find out that Ali's elderly and sick parents were inside the house, alone and unconcerned. They were migrants from the Visayas and when they arrived in Niog, they built a small shack at the back of the house that was built inside the land of their Caviteño relatives.

'Strangers!' 'Freeloaders!' what I repeatedly hear from his aunt. Ali cried while arguing. I also wept at the scene because I pitied the image of an older brother carrying his younger brother and defending himself in response to scolding. What I witnessed was more real compared to the actors crying on telenovelas. After that scene, I decided to befriend Ali and become close to him. When he once bought at the store a five-peso lard while he was still carrying his brother, I took the chance of introducing myself and talking to him. Since the nights with Evelyn were over, Ali became my new storyteller. I found out he was an out-of-school youth and that for him was good enough.

Ali showed me that many young people in Niog who grew up in poverty dreamt of becoming a factory worker. That period was the beginning of the time when Cavite was infested with factories due to the established Export Processing Zones. There were many like Ali who focused more on looking inside the factory as a means of livelihood than studying inside the classroom. So Ali, like other Niog residents, didn't go to school again and chose to work inside the factory. One day, he was very happy to tell me that he had been hired as a worker in a ceramics factory with other Niog residents who were once my troop-mates. And since he was going to be pulled away by the physical labour, our long conversations have become seldom until the end of my second and last vacation in Niog where I never even had a chance to say goodbye.

There were times when I was in college, I would occasionally come back to Niog during special occasions. Sometimes it was during a fiesta or on the birthday of an old friend. Every time I came back, I heard new information. Annie and Venus, Aunt Zeny's nieces, had a family of their own and they both worked in Japan. It broke my heart to find out that Inying was dead because of an illness caused by heavy drinking. He was found one day not breathing in his shack. I was excited to see Ali again and congratulated him when he was promoted as a supervisor in the factory. I was happy to find out the stories of my fellow troops having girlfriends and getting married for good. I'd smile to find out that Joy was been married, built his own family, and found livelihood for his future child with Evelyn.

I always brought something home every time I visited Niog. Aunt Zeny would never forget to buy me school supplies every time I went home to Cembo. I didn't consider it payment in exchange for helping them with the sales. I liked to think they did it because they considered me their child. And I always remembered her for the good that she had done and I was forever grateful to her whenever we would meet today. Of course, I brought back to Cembo all of the experiences I gained there and they are useful to this day. From More and Champion Blue, I'm doing my doctorate now in Marlboro. I can still play the guitar and sing in front of drunkards. Most of all, I have more people like Inying and Ali and to this day, I talk to, listen to, and consider them my friends.

I never went to my father's town, Imus, Cavite. I didn't even try. I never saw him there nor searched for him either. But it was in Niog that I discovered the experience of having a parent, a friend, and a loved one. These experiences gave depth to my character. The lack of support from my departed father was filled up by my new family, friends and loved ones who gave strength to the recesses of my being, especially while growing up. I'm not a kid anymore so I learnt a hard lesson in life, standing up for my own decisions.

Repaks

I came to Cembo without any friends or acquaintances other than my cousins and siblings. So I had high hopes before the beginning of classes, and because it was a vacation, I would make new friends in the village. It will eventually happen but through violent situations that will test my bravery as a man. The reason is, I will be caught up in a brawl with a boy named Randy Almonte who always annoyed me whenever I passed by their street in Ipil to visit my god-brother Ronald.

I didn't know why this fool played a trick on me—I guess it's obvious that I'm new to this place, and being small looked weak to him. Every time he did this, I actually went home, my chest almost exploding in resentment. I didn't want Mama to know because I knew she won't do anything about it either. I was also afraid that Mama might fight back and tell Randy's parents about it and the mess would escalate, which would only further boost Randy to call me a cry baby and a snitch.

So one day, when he provoked me again as I passed by, the pent-up anger exploded. I felt Randy was harassing me because I was small and when I couldn't stand it anymore, I challenged him to a one-on-one.

We fist-fought under the narra tree on Narra St. Using my knowledge of watching lots of kung fu movies, I formed a Karate Kid stance and immediately hit him on the face with the first blow, dropping him on his bicycle that was blocking me.

The madman fell and never recovered. I continued kicking him with the 'karate' until somebody stepped in to stop us. After the tournament, I saw some kids, including Boy and Marcial, raise my hand because they said I won over their bully. I was told that they knew karate. If they only knew how bad my chest was pounding when I challenged this bully and the pounding that came after that on my chest, that made me continuously attack Randy. My knees were trembling as well. If they only knew it was pure luck and honestly how would I be aware of karate? I just imitated what I saw on TV.

That's where I found new friends, Boy and Marcial. I would also leave them one day when Dodie challenged me to play basketball. The ball hit me as I verbally fought his complaints about the game. I was turning my back on him. I quickly turned around and jumped over the surprised Dodie and did the 'karate' again. After the second tournament, his clothes were torn and scratched. I think he was still in shock. Second luck. A few days after this scene, Dodie's playmates will become my permanent childhood friends from that basketball game. They were Andheng, Ato, Empoy, Randy Kuba, Butch, James, Percy, Allan and of course, Dodie and his eldest brother Bong. We were all from Acacia. My friendship with Boy and Marcial grew apart eventually because they lived in Narra, and I wasn't able to go there as I was hanging out with the kids in Acacia.

Our hangout was a bakery opposite the village's basketball court during the holidays. We would also be in the company of seniors hanging out in the area. This den will be known as Rancho Pogi. But if Rancho Pogi is the name that even the older people in our group will call that place, we, the young kids, would be known as the Easy Boys. Butch came up with the name to challenge another rival group.

There used to be some angsty youth groups in our place called the Yankees. They were older than us but they also had members of our age who often bossed around the streets. Randy is one of them but on the day I kicked him with my karate, which I didn't know! We wanted to fight one-on-one even if we're not street brawlers. It is more accurate to say we only needed backup if ever something picks on a fight. Even though I still feel today, if a fight ever came up and someone hit us, we wouldn't be able to fight back either because when I met them, we didn't do anything every time it got dark but sit around a campfire and tell stories in a vacant lot next to a basketball court full of uncut grass. Sometimes we would build a cottage on the side of the vacant lot and here we would experiment with eating and cooking a dish from ingredients that we stole from our own kitchens. We would tell stories about our personal experiences and our youthful dreams until we felt sleepy and went home.

But if we had the greatest opponent, it was when we hit a boy named Alex because he called us uncircumcised when he got upset after being teased. The Easy Boys knocked down the lone opponent. After all, he was annoyed that he emphasized the real situation of some of us. So we got very annoyed and alas, poor Alex, was left helpless. He received the hardest hit from the uncircumcised. And I was one of them.

One day, the bulldozers arrived. Several mountains were blown up to penetrate Kalayaan Avenue towards C-5. The basketball court as well as the vacant lot were gone. The houses shrunk. Some families had their houses ransacked, and being paid for by the government, moved elsewhere. Dodie and Bong moved to another house. Even Butch's family. James didn't go out much and focused on studying at the marine school. The bakery and our den were affected by the rampage and widening of Kalayaan Avenue. And the former Acacia Street has become Kalayaan Avenue. The rest of us who were left behind witnessed all of these changes. We would only get used to this when all of us stepped into college and left behind our childhood selves and the Easy Boys. Our passions also changed. Here we will be known as Repaks.

In the early 1990s, we felt that we were too old to engage in children's fights. We would become passionate about rock music. Every Saturday, we would hang out at any of Andheng, Ato, or Percy's house for a sound trip. While learning to drink alcohol, we would listen over and over again to the music of the bands Bon Jovi, White Lion, Nirvana, Metallica, Pearl Jam, Extreme, and many more. Because some of the bands mentioned have done concerts here in the Philippines, and some of us have been to these concerts, we will all join in a band.

This was followed by our dream of forming our own band. But we must first learn to play instruments. I first learned the guitar and Aunt Bing was my first teacher. And when I was able to play more than ten songs, after 'bleeding my nose' in the *1001 Song Book*, many song hits, and 'stealing' some hooking and zipping techniques from some guitarists I encountered, I became more confident to join in playing the guitar and singing with the old people of Rancho Pogi every time there was a drinking session. I was even nicknamed Bon Jovi because they often requested me to play the songs of his band. They also liked that my voice is close to the timbre of rock vocalists. It's because I have a husky voice.

Our passion for rock music intensified when the alternative rock scene exploded in the Philippines. Eraserheads and other underground bands paved the way for alternative rock to enter mainstream rock that was once dominated by foreign bands. LA 105 station will take the lead in playing alternative rock music by underground bands. The station will introduce the segment 'Power Pick that will play selected great demo songs by new bands who want to be named. They will surpass the previously more popular rock station NU 107. Because of this, we were encouraged to fulfil our dream of forming a band and becoming famous one day.

The spacious bakery where we used to hangout has become an alley. When we come back from our classes in college, we will all go straight here and wait for everyone. And since band culture was a hit in those days, my childhood friends will also learn to play the guitar and other instruments. Andheng, Empoy, and I were on the guitar. We will assign Ato to the bass guitar. Percy loves the drums. Kuba and Allan, our groupies, were among others hanging out.

The day came when almost everyone knew how to play all of the instruments, and Andheng will tell the story of being busted by the person he is courting because the girl already has a boyfriend. Because of this, we will both write the song 'Mahal kita', meaning I love you.

The song became a hit with the elderly. Because of this, we were encouraged to really build a band. We started with a contribution of fifty pesos to watch one night of Filipino bands at Amoranto Stadium in Quezon City. There, I first saw Eraserheads (who were still rocked by punks on stage), The Youth (dubbed Nirvana of the Philippines), Alamid (who sang their hit song 'Your Love'), and the veteran group, The Dawn.

After that evening, from the love song 'Mahal Kita' we will create anthemic songs and always with a streak of social relevance like 'Dyaryo' (Newspaper) and 'Walang Kasiyahan' (No Fun). The band is complete. Me on vocals, Empoy on lead guitar, Andheng on rhythm guitar, Ato on bass guitar, and Percy on drums. Kuba and Allan were our sound technicians and Bernie, one of the old men, was our instrument repairer.

The first Cembo band named by the seniors hanging out in our den is complete. They called us Repaks. We just lacked real electronic instruments and managers. But we didn't have money and we were just broke students.

Since it was a vacation at that time and we were almost always together to rehearse with the old guitars of the elderly, we thought of making a drum set. We collected gas containers, small and large as well as a dos-por-dos scrap wood. We will work together to shape and nail our drum set. We built small containers for the snare and tom-toms, and large containers for the bass drum. The clapper is a rounded wire with bottle caps. The same is placed on top of the container that will serve as snare drums. Wood and rubber from slingshots were used for the drum pedal. We formed container drums and in the evening, Percy eagerly beat it as we played our own compositions and fundraised songs.

Everyone was overjoyed. It looked like we were the Beatles playing that night on the side of Kalayaan Avenue and people passing by were watching. Some are wondering; some are excited. That scene was new in Cembo. In a few moments, someone will be buying beer from the old men watching by and the band's first jamming will be about drinking and singing. That night, we declared that we were already a band. But we know, we still need to learn the real electrical instruments of a real band. Because at the same time as that first jamming, we also dreamt of meeting and hearing the songs we created outside the Rancho Pogi.

When classes resumed, we saved our money to rent a band studio. Percy even pawned some of his jewellery given to him by his parents who were working abroad. All of these just to have a 150–300-peso payment at a band studio in Pasay where we will rehearse with electrical instruments and hear the sound of our music on a live recording. In fact, we spent more time experimenting with sounds every time we went to that band studio. It's funny for us kids who were excited about our new toys that we didn't even know how to use. Percy was beating louder and louder on the drums as we tuned in and seasoned the voice and guitars. We were also often surprised by the sudden feedback of guitars and microphones because they were like horses that haven't yet been tamed, because we were not yet used to handling them! Rehearsals were always noisy and funnily annoying. We would leave the studio happy because we were able to show off our new skills in playing even though there wasn't really a single polished song. But it happened one day and our polished songs increased when suddenly a blessing came.

It was when Elvis arrived and met us. Jokes apart, Elvis was really his name. And he also loved our music. Elvis was over thirty when we were just nineteen- and twenty-year-olds. I invited him to join the band because he said he knew how to play the keyboard. Most of all, Elvis just got off the ship as a seaman. He brought lots of talent with him. He was a good manager as well. And that's exactly what happened. Elvis was our keyboardist and manager. One day, he would invite us to buy instruments from guitars, distortions, and real drum sets! He really funded it. After all, he suggested changing the name of the band from Repaks to Seagulls, which is said to be the name of the ship he boarded. Of course, the 'council of elders' hanging out with us thought the name was lame. We too found it uncool. At the right time, I told our Manager Elvis, and that we'd still prefer Repaks. He was easy to talk to so the name of the band wasn't changed. But on one condition. I have to create many more songs. Because if we really want to be famous, we have to be able to record songs that will become an album. And I would even create songs with the help of bands.

Although we had different musical influences before we formed the band, the band didn't have any problem with the lyrics and melody of the songs I wrote. The lyrics were often full of meaning and the rock melodies were radio-friendly. The sounds of pop, new wave, and hard rock have lyrics that are full of social relevance. Even the love songs. They crossed all lines, spectrums, and ages. And since we already had a permanent rehearsal area—on the rooftop of Elvis' house on the side of Kalayaan Avenue—and the instruments were complete. There was no reason for us not to rehearse. Every night we would do it after our classes. As a result of these rehearsals, we were able to polish five songs for our album.

We recorded from morning to night. Cassette tapes were still in vogue back then and eight tracks was the cheapest recording. After each record, we would listen to it immediately. It was bad. The sound did not live up to our expectations. Maybe it could pass for those who wanted to do a sound trip but for the meticulous, the mix of the sound engineer was so dirty he even profited from us because he added costs per hour from the first rate he agreed with Elvis. We weren't satisfied but nothing could be done. We had to hurry because some of our contemporaries in other villages were already ahead of us, playing their music in LA 105.

The next day, carrying a box of donuts, the band went to the radio station and handed over the demo tape. Two weeks later one morning, Percy was shouting in front of our house because one of the songs, 'No Fun', had been playing on the radio. Ato, who heard the song while riding in the jeep, almost went to the middle of the street just to shout to the whole world that our song was already being played. It became the station's Power Pick, and we knew it would be played again in the afternoon. I never went to class that afternoon. The others also hurried home from their classes. At five o'clock in the afternoon, when it was played again and for the first time we heard the hard-earned song on the radio, everyone, young or old, shouted for joy inside Ato's house, which was our assembly area. It didn't matter if we had found the recording bad. The important thing is the songs we used to sing on our hangouts were played on the radio.

I remember almost choking with excitement. We all jumped with joy as if we'd become famous. But that's how we became famous in the village. After that, we were invited to play in the Junior Senior prom, birthdays, weddings, and fiestas. What's only missing was the last day of a wake. We had gigs in Cavite, Caloocan, Batangas, and other districts in Makati. And man, we were always drunk because everywhere we sang there was partying and drinking. We were always full. And there were lots of girls to meet. We were becoming popular among other groups hanging out in Cembo. We sang songs to them, free of charge. At this point, Elvis has already figured out how to profit. So when the next vacation of 1995 came, he invited us to tour the Bicol province.

Elvis allegedly sent the demo tape to all the radio stations in the town of Legazpi. We would go there to try to play in hotels and get paid. We wasted no time, and one holiday afternoon, we would work together to cram instruments and ourselves into a small and an old jeep owned by Elvis' brother-in-law. We were like sardines inside. We endured this for about fifteen hours of the trip. Our drummer Percy wasn't there. He was obliged to take summer classes at school so we went to Legazpi with a missing drummer. We would get there one morning to spend two weeks on vacation and a gig.

We lived in a vacant house in a village in Legazpi called Bigaa. It belonged to Elvis' aunt. A bungalow with an adjoining hut that—we could not understand why—had no stairs even though its floor was high. And in the very dark of the night, in the countryside, along with the stories of Elvis' relatives about the ghosts in the area, we would avoid opening the door of the house and peeing outside to avoid the stairless hut. It scared me. Even the house we stayed in had a man's bedroom as well as a bathroom so we would squeeze into a room and always just take a shower outside. We took turns pumping water from a well. We avoided taking a bath in the big restroom because it was dank and dark but when the time came to shit, we faced our fears and pooped quickly. Sometimes, I would see some newly washed briefs with yellow patches. Somebody jerked off.

We first had to rehearse to audition at a hotel. What happens now that we don't have a drummer? We had some trainees who were recommended to play the drums but they didn't pass for our performances. It was this time that I really cursed Percy's summer class. Our only saving grace was that we heard on the first day we were here that a radio station in that town playing not just one, but all five songs we recorded! We were known in the town of Legazpi especially after we were interviewed one night by a Radio DJ. In that interview we will say that we all just came from one place and have been friends for a long time. My pogi points that could've made me more attracted just dropped when the DJ described me as having a 'big voice even if small' while Ato was described as a *tisoy*—a mestizo. So after the interview, the station's telephone will ring one after another for the female listeners to look for Ato. Some of them will even go to the studio, a few minutes after the interview! By the way, they will leave immediately without talking to Ato because Ato isn't really a tisoy.

After the interview, our songs were played every day on that station. They also included greetings with the names of our former DJ friends—after Elvis got very drunk on the night of the interview. Other bands in that area will also hear of our presence. One afternoon, a local band named Apocalipse would come to our place and invite us to jam. At first we would proudly play some compositions to show off. But we will also be quickly stunned by the fact that the crazy rockers play their songs. The cover songs and the sound of their compositions are pure metal rock. Fast guitar fingers! The jaws of the Repaks dropped. We will be obliged to befriend them, which will be fun and deep in the end, because they are not arrogant unlike other bands that want to be famous. Ouch!

In a few days, during our first week in the village of Bigaa, we will receive invitations to play. But we will never step into the 'hotel that pays', which was Elvis's plan in the first place.

Our first gig was at a kindergarten graduation at a small school opposite where we were staying. Since we will be borrowing the drummer of the band Apocalipse, we will also include them in the billing as the front act. We admit they had better playing skills. Our rock was more attuned to pop so we were better understood by many. Because theirs is heavy metal that is really for rockers and head-bangers. The little kids from kinder will better understand our songs as compared to their *raaaaaawwwwr* performance.

The second gig was the miting de avance of local politicians. At a farm. It was tough but since we are still itching to be famous, we will let it go. We were the first to play. Because people could hear me on the radio, someone was still singing along with me. There are those who will approach me, a young woman, telling me to 'go home.' The vocalist of Apocalipse was quick to stop me because the woman was said to come from a family of aswangs—like those vampires or viscera-suckers in the West. Shit! I just put up with the More cigarette—this cigarette will be our 'official cigar' for the rest of our stay in the Bicol province—that was served to us on the farm with white tin plates and blue lining on the side. Showing again the *raaaaaawwwwr!* of the Apocalipse, people suddenly became preoccupied with various things. We would find out that the audience were friends of the vocalist's father who was running for elections as village captain.

After these two gigs, Elvis admitted to himself that we didn't really go to Bicol to make money. But he will still continue the Repaks tour. And so that he could recover completely, a week later we would take the instruments on a passenger motorboat to go to the real place where Elvis grew up. San Ramon Island, the largest of the three Rapu-Rapu islands. From the port of Legazpi, we will sail the ocean for three hours until we reach the island. There on that island, we will be greeted as rockstars by the neighbours of Elvis' family. Only once were there visitors from Manila among them. And it's a band!

The supposed rock stars were famished. We immediately devoured the *adobong baka* that was served to us. When we were full, the family would admit that we ate pickled turtles. It was all right. We weren't disgusted at all. It really tasted like beef. And honestly, we missed a week of kwaw fish, vegetables, and Bicol express that Elvis' aunt cooked for us during our stay in Bigaa. After being fed with turtles as our starting menu in San Ramon, it will be followed by a native chicken tinola, lobster, various fish, and *ayaw*—a dish made from dog—in the following days of our stay on the island.

Back then, my stomach was still stuffy especially since I couldn't control my greed. So on the first day I visited the toilet of Elvis' house, I was confused as to how to poop in their toilet, which was a hole on the floor. Because I had just seen such a toilet for the first time, and because I was not used to squatting like a frog. Stepping on the lip of the toilet, I immediately applied my butt to its lip and stretched my leg against the cement floor, my thigh and leg. Actually, nothing came out. I can't push it out! My thighs and legs were filled with the soil and sand on the floor. The fools burst into laughter when I recounted my 'toilet adventure' to them. Even better, Empoy, when he once fed us lobster at Elvis's brother's house on the neighbouring island, 'behaved like a king' and made a throne on top of a large rock by the coconut trees. Success!

Everywhere we went, someone greeted us, and somebody introduced themselves. We looked like artists but we didn't become artists. We were all sociable and pure cowboys. So we became more congenial, Andheng and I in particular, who often greeted them, especially when we met the most beautiful and whitest maiden of the island that one night. Andheng and I were drunk. We waited for the store to close while lying on the moored boat. But we were both really stupid. The girl didn't notice us. So nothing happened either. We both fell asleep on the boat because we were tipsy and busted.

Because Elvis' family was the richest on the island and they were a family of politicians, it really helped us know a lot of people on the island. In fact, the electricity of every home came from the large generator that his family owned. They were paid one peso per bulb every night. On the last night we played in their small plaza to show our gratitude for their warm welcome; there were no women, old or young, in front of the stage, aside from the island men drinking on the side. They preferred to watch and listen while looking down at the windows of their houses surrounding the plaza. I'm not even sure if they understood what we're playing and if they liked the sound. To be sure, it was only then that their place lit up when they didn't have to pay for electricity. And maybe, they proved that 'aliens' could also play.

After that vacation, our paths changed. We needed to graduate to have something to prove someday. We would rarely rehearse until we split up a few days before the beginning of the new school year when we got back to Cembo.

I transferred to another college because I had decided to become a teacher. My bandmates would also focus on studying. Elvis boarded the ship again. With the exception of living in Bataan due to marriage, we would not be able to hear about him. Although there were still a few opportunities for me to create songs, the muse of writing continued to pull me along as our instruments gathered dust on the rooftop where we used to rehearse. Eventually, we heard that the drum set was brought home to Elvis' place. One day, the bass guitar was stolen from Empoy's house and Andheng was going to sell his guitar.

Although we felt sad when we abandoned the instruments, it did not last long because of our busy schedules as students. Time will pass when everyone will graduate, they will all have new jobs and build their own families. They will become compadres and godfathers to their children. Sometimes they will go out for a drink. Ato and Empoy will become seamen. Andheng will work for a brokerage. Percy is now a radio technologist at a hospital. Kuba will work at a well-known mall while Allan will be a government employee. I will be a full-fledged teacher.

When we tried to hold a reunion—also at the urging of new bands and the young people hanging out at Cembo—we would once again play our songs. Fortunately, the screams were louder due to the yelling of the drinkers, so they never noticed—or perhaps they ignored it—that we were hanging out playing our songs again. There are times when I forget the lyrics of the other songs we made while they forget the strokes and beats on the guitar and drums. The riot was back again. It's like we're starting all over. But the music just kept going. Abundant with silly and foolish audiences! But most importantly, they joined us in singing these songs. That's what matters. They still know our songs.

When we want to relive the stories of some friends who wonder why we didn't become famous, we always brag that 'at least, we became famous in Bicol!' or 'at least, we made our own songs!' On occasions like this, while looking at the aging face of my bandmates, I would say to myself: 'Once upon a time, here in Cembo, in the company of true friends and experience, we, the Repaks, were the first band to be loved!'

And I'm sure, even if our playing skills have gone, even if we don't really become famous and even if our songs aren't fully known all over the country, even if we lose our instruments, we will continue to look for stories and experiences of our once beloved band. We will continue to play in the depths of our being.

Rakenrol!

The Convent

When I was in my third year of high school, I knew that Mama's biggest problem was how to put me through college. But I wasn't serious about it. There were too many things happening back then that made me think of these problems. It was the heyday of MC Hammer and Vanilla Ice, and of course, the Universal Motion Dancers. The 1990s were just beginning. Dancing to the beats was the norm. There were many boys who wanted to play the guitar because of the very popular song 'More Than Words'. Everywhere there were parties set up by groups who had a mobile sound system business—they would 'mobile' as what it was called back then. They would earn 10–30 pesos from entrance fees from young people who were excited to dance, flirt, court, and ready to come home a 'de-virginized' hoe. Inside the homes and video shops, everyone betted on how Super Mario and Luigi would quickly save the princess on the family computer.

One organization back then would introduce me to think of the future. But before I could totally accept it in my humanity, I needed to strengthen my spirituality.

The group's name was the Marian Youth Movement (MYM). Every Wednesday, after class, they would become Batman and Robin arriving in-tandem as brothers from their convents; it is only now that I found out that nuns aren't the only people that live in convents. The brothers wore polo-barong that didn't match. Sometimes they wore very black and sometimes very white tops, with matching black pants and shoes; there's one brother who was wearing a shoe with broken soles. Their clean-cut hair looked like they were licked by cows. One carried a Bible while the other carried a guitar. They often wore wooden crosses as necklaces.

At first, I would take a peek at the group's activities. When they would sing 'I am Happy', I'd laugh so hard at their corny song and at the other students and some classmates who sang in the group. And what was lamer was that they would include hand gestures in their songs. There were like huge birds that flap their wings whenever they sing the song 'The Birds'.

The members of MYM would meet in an empty classroom. The year levels were mixed from the freshmen to the seniors. Mrs Violeta Perando, my class adviser, was also the adviser—called animator—of MYM. At that time, aside from seeing that most of my notebooks were full of drawings, one would never be proud of the grades that came out of my card. To be frank, if the school didn't have a choral competition, I wouldn't have a group that would make me cool and noticeable by my girl classmates. So that my class standing will be better to my class adviser and be close to the girls at my school, I joined the MYM.

The corniness I felt while singing in the group was nothing compared to me singing the action songs. I felt shame and corniness bursting in my whole existence while singing and whispering along with them with a forced smile. Aside from the two songs that I mentioned, there was a long repertoire of charismatic songs that the MYM brothers brought for the motivational part of the session. There was this song called 'Making Melodies in my Heart', one with 'Thumbs in! Elbows up! Feet apart!' until we reached the 'Tongues out' and 'Go around' and 'I'm Leaning on the Lord's Side', and many others.

There was also a mellow song that made us tearful; it felt like our soul will be lifted up to heaven.

All this was followed by a lecture about the word of God, and it was connected to our current lives as students. There was that one where they mentioned the evil brought by the changes of our bodies and emotions in our youth; how to avoid temptations and sin; and most of all, asking for forgiveness from the Lord. The two brothers were abundant with quotations that gave inspiration, and careful meditation to anyone who wanted a new life close to the Lord. And because Marian was the first word that would be seen in the name of their group, they venerated the Blessed Virgin Mary as the only path connecting to Jesus. As what their motto said: To Jesus through Mary. That's why the group was always full of activities like praying the rosary and singing praises to the Virgin Mary.

One style of the MYM brothers was to play on the emotions of the students, especially the part where they would introduce the importance of loving parents. They would tell the students to close their eyes. They would turn off the lights in the classroom—because most meetings would extend until dusk—and let silence enclose the whole classroom. When there was no more noise, one brother would strum a sad melody on the guitar. Sometimes instrumental; sometimes accompanied it with a hum. Then a cold God-like voice would begin speaking. A soft inviting voice. He would begin with a few questions about the existence of life such as: 'Do you know why we exist?' or 'Have you ever asked why God chose you to live in this borrowed life?' And then this question was followed by asking about the sins we've done to our parents. 'Why do you have to answer back and stamp annoyingly in front of your parents while they're teaching you a lesson?' Or, 'Why can't you follow them?' And my most favourite—while secretly smirking—was the part where they would 'kill' the parents! 'As you go home, in the distance you will see your house filled with many lights and many people, and you felt something wrong inside. You walked faster and when you arrived at the door, your parents were inside the casket...'

A few students would start sobbing at the phrase 'filled with many lights and many people' and then, by the end of that sob story with a twist 'your parents were inside the casket', the whole room will be filled with the sound of my classmates' cries. This would level up when the brothers said, 'You weren't even able to ask for forgiveness to them before you saw them inside the casket.' It was in this part where the wailing became a riot that filled the room. Sweat—because even the electric fan was turned off, and I don't know why—mixed with phlegm and tears. The 'macho' guys like me swore and chuckled silently.

It was very corny. The moral lesson was to follow one's parents because otherwise it might be too late to say sorry for these 'sinful, smart-mouthed and tantrum-throwing children'. And then, the lights would be turned on and glare at those teary, awakened eyes. Tears and mucus could still be seen on the cheeks of those children when a brother suddenly played the guitar with another closing action song and ends with a closing prayer. Then we waited for a new character to 'die' in a session next Wednesday.

I would master all of the action songs, rosary prayers, playing of student's emotions with a mix of their tears, sweat and mucus out of wailing, and all other corniness that came with these activities when I became an MYM brother after graduating from high school.

When I was in my third year of high school before the summer vacation, I joined an overnight retreat organized by the MYM, which included my classmate and friend Rommel— the son of my adviser—because I wasn't able to join another classmate, Antonino, who had an eye injury at home. In short, I was Antonino's replacement. We were four delegates in the retreat. It was evening when we went and searched Moonwalk, Parañaque. We rode the wrong jeep because we had reached Moonwalk, Las Piñas. For a few hours, we were lost before reaching Barangay Merville in Parañaque and inside, and we were able to reach Barangay Moonwalk where there was an exclusive well-off community where the Holy Eucharist Parish stood and was called a 'convent' of the brothers because this is where they lived. MYM's spiritual director, Fr Matt Garcia was at the height of his speech when we arrived. Even though we were late, we were lucky to still join the group sharing.

Rommel and I were separated from our companions to join other delegates from other schools. There was an activity where our group needed to share our struggles in life. For a long time, I never shared my private struggles in life with anyone; even the fact that I grew up without a father. What I felt back then was if I told this to other people, even to new acquaintances, it was like revealing what was lacking in my personality. I felt this because I didn't grow up like them who had a complete family and bought anything they wanted. But after listening to their life stories, I warmed up and opened a part of myself to them. I realized that our struggles were never far apart from each other. I listened to them and they listened to me. We felt each other's presence without judgment. And it was accepted at that time that only God could heal the wounds of our lives. On that occasion, I felt my openness as a person to others and to God.

With the experience of that retreat, which was very different from my experiences with vices and partying with friends and classmates, I declared to myself that I would be a serious member of MYM. At that same retreat, I learnt that anyone who wished to enter as an MYM brother would be exempted from studying. I immediately saw this path as my ticket to a scholarship and help with Mama's problems.

When I heard at the MYM retreat that anyone who passed as a brother would have a scholarship, I seized the opportunity to become a candidate. Simultaneous to the offer of free education, was the willingness to live inside the convent in Parañaque for a whole year and leave studying to perform catechism in various schools in Manila. I prepared myself for these conditions. Even if I stopped studying for a year, it was a good decision. Let the others go to college first because they were well-off. I would follow soon. To me, this was my one-way ticket to college. And this was the only way to lighten the burden on my mother's shoulder who always supported me and my brother. So when the vacation came after I graduated from high school, I was one of the ten candidates for brotherhood who would spend more than a month in the convent to be trained and selected for a religious life. It was April 1992.

Brother Lorenzo Maria Jarin became my name in the convent. We were obliged to change our names to a saint's name and append the name of the Virgin Mary as we became a candidate. It was a symbol of our new persona. A person who is a close worker of God. We read a book containing stories about the lives of saints. Here we chose the beloved saint who would be our patron. Names of foreign saints replaced the real names of my comrades. Out of a sense of patriotism, I chose the name San Lorenzo Ruiz as my new name. The only Filipino saint back then.

Twelve of us became candidates for brotherhood. We all came from around Manila. Some came from Tondo, Sampaloc, and Quezon City. We were both from Makati, me and Angel Lopez—who would later become Brother Bernard and one of my closest associates in the convent with Francis and Martin. At the same time, the MYM leadership seemed to be experimenting. They planned to have sisters too whom they called Christophorus. They would participate with us in training. Everyone came from around Manila. One of them was my high school classmate, Julie. All of us—when we became candidates during that 1992 vacation—were only sixteen or seventeen years old. All mostly new high school graduates. Everyone dreamt of a religious life, forever.

With the help of the elder brothers, we began our training. It was explained that at the end of the training—and if we passed—there was a law of stay-out or stay-in in the convent. The stay-outs were the brothers and all the sisters who lived outside the convent and were educated by their parents.

In between their studies, they would act as catechists in the schools that were set up for them. They would only go to the convent on Saturday and Sunday to report and share with the stay-in companions. The stay-ins were brothers who would stay for a full year in the convent and first stop studying to become MYM scholars in college next year. They would go full time to the schools assigned to them to work in the apostolate that we called catechism in high schools.

But before this, they were trained to strengthen their mind and actions. It was heavy discipline. You will fear God, for God and only God should be on the mind. And every day, even though Pinoy Big Brother was not yet popular, the pressure of training revealed the true traits of everyone that were initially covered up by the posture of 'immediate holiness' for the sake of passing.

We slept early and woke up early. There was a reading in the Breviary of some revelations of God when we woke up and before we went to sleep. We served as a sacristan at every Mass. There was only a designated time to speak with each other. When we talked to the sister, there had to be two arms away from them. Loud laughter was forbidden. Loud conversations were also forbidden unless we were singing songs related to the love of God. Of course, love songs were forbidden. We prayed the rosary every day. It was a good thing we didn't continue to pray the rosary at a very slow pace with our arms outstretched. At the second mystery, our arms, hands and body cramped. And my favourite—while asleep, we'd tie a rosary around our hands to ward off the 'temptation of masturbation' as a man.

Chastity. Poverty. Obedience. As with those who attended the seminary, this was the sum total of the principles we had to live by. Live without malice and away from worldly desires. Avoid the life of luxury. Be humble and always follow the commandments of the church and the MYM fraternity.

Some said goodbye at the very beginning when they realized that they preferred life outside the convent. Other left without their goodbyes. They had issues. Upon awakening, there was one who saw the beads of the rosary scattered beside the bed. Someone confessed that he had not avoided the temptation when the fellow man stepped aside and began to 'have something to do with his what' and he let it go. Of course, they both should've said their goodbye. There was also somebody called the 'bad boy' of the convent who resembled Robin Padilla when walking. He was described by the sisters as bad-mouthed and when disgusted with their comrades, swore a lot. He was hot-headed and always stirred up a fight. It was me.

In the first few weeks of training, I appeared irritable with the situation. I was often bored. There were some candidates I didn't agree with right away. I thought of them as queer. They were friendly to the point that they wanted to make me look like I was the bully and the angsty boy in the crowd, and my opinions or anything I said couldn't be ignored. I thought highly of myself. I don't know, but that's what the older brothers observed about me. And all this could be the basis for me not passing the training as a brother candidate. I passed through chastity and poverty, yet I failed in obedience.

One day, after we were given a weekend day-off and returned to our families, I arrived in the afternoon at the convent as if wondering at the strange kindness in the conversation of the candidates I had met. By evening, the older brothers called me to a room. They surrounded me when they said: 'Life in the convent is not for you.' My world collapsed. I shivered and soon my tears welled up. The situation at home immediately came to my mind. Penniless. Good for nothing. There was no future. There was no lesson. My only ticket to go to college slipped through my palm because of my arrogance. And I needed to make them understand me.

I told the truth. That being a brother would be my only passport to stepping into college. My mother didn't have a regular job, and we had nothing else to look forward to. I promised that I would change my behaviour. Be humble. Maybe I really had a talent for being pitied, because they gave me another chance! They said they saw that I had potential. It was a pity if it was not available.

By the end of the training throughout that vacation period, of the twelve who wanted to be brothers, only six of us were fortunate enough to become full MYM brothers. The sisters all stayed out. And two sisters each were matched to each brother with six designated schools to be assigned to an apostolate. Six of us went bald as a symbol of humility. And in the summer of 1992, during the Blessed Sacrament of the church, all six of us swore to God that no one of us would leave and we would all someday, after being brothers, enter the seminary and become full priests so more people could be evangelized by the words and love of God.

In the apostolate, I wore a white—sometimes black—polo, black pants and old black shoes, baby-oil polished hair, with a

wooden crucifix necklace, and most of all, carried a guitar across
my body. I would take a jeep, bus or sometimes the train to
many schools under the heat of the sun, sweating as I entered
the classrooms, and going straight to sharing the Word of
God. It was a lucky day when my teacher-animator at school
had a new salary and would give me a snack before going
home. But I could never rely on this. So I would often come
home to the convent late at night and be very hungry. Often
I went to more than two schools. So the fun I experienced
interacting with MYM member students in each school was a
big thing. It took away my tiredness and I believe this was also
how my MYM brothers and sisters hoped to feel. But it was
always difficult to get started.

There were schools I visited that had almost no student
members. Former members had either graduated or lost
interest after vacation. Nor was it different from teacher-
animators. There were some who wanted to stop the extra
work of mentoring at MYM due to a lot of academic work and
teaching, although there were still some who were active. Some
schools eventually suspended the organizing of MYM because
their principals weren't Catholic. Almost all of the schools we
went to were public.

As I have said before, I was only sixteen at the time. It
was a huge test of faith because as the brother-in-charge of
these schools, it was my responsibility to revive the 'dying' of
the MYM in schools and to further spread those who were
still active. Fortunately, with God's guidance, I developed
my self-confidence and discovered that I had the charisma
to communicate with a wide variety of people. Regardless of
their age. I persuaded many students to join MYM. I also had
many returning members. Singing and humour became my
investment to persuade. I also conducted activities in which the
members themselves spoke their views and interpretations on

a particular portion of God's Word. I did this so that everyone could feel that they were part of every meeting. And I'm sure they felt it too because I was able to make them sing more at the same time without being embarrassed. It even got to the point where they were ahead in sharing even without me insisting them to do it.

This was even more evident because whenever general gatherings of schools with MYM—retreats, seminar-workshops, and Christmas parties—were held, the six schools assigned to us were some of the schools with the most student members and animators who attended and participated in activities. Events like this had given me invaluable inspiration to further improve as a brother and to enjoy the sacredness of living inside and outside the convent. This happened for a time but later on, I wasn't inspired enough to stay inside the convent.

There were events inside that led me to break the rules. The concept of being obedient to similar institutions I entered is, at least, not complaining and questioning whatever is being complained about you. I have always known that my personality was not in harmony with this system. In short, there were commands I did not follow. Again, I failed in obedience.

There was a practice within the convent that if you committed an offence—not doing the prescribed activities such as sleeping late, not praying the rosary, singing love songs, waking up late, not turning off the lights at night and electric fan in the morning, fighting, being too close to sisters or courting them, and many others—and you have done it three times, then there were heavy penalties: you will be bald, your companions will not talk to you, you will serve the brothers and sisters food when gathering, wash what they eat and the heaviest for me, wash their dirty clothes. The end of this punishment depended on whether the leadership was convinced of a learning in the person bearing the punishment.

These penalties were imposed on me a second time. At first, I did it all to be received inside the convent. Because after I promised to change from my arrogant self just to be allowed to be a brother, I had to go through the penalties. In the middle of what I think was my blossoming career as an energetic brother, at the same time, I forgot one morning to turn off the electric fan, I sang love songs one afternoon, and stayed up one night because I wanted to write something to say for the future apostolate. All of this was reported to Father Matt by an older brother who watched over our daily activities while inside the convent.

I did not accept the punishment imposed on me because I couldn't accept that what I had done was a mistake. I was overwhelmed by what they said was my offence this time. I didn't consider them a big sin other than simply not following them. I just forgot to follow. It's different to miss out on disobedience really. All of this I justified but everything ended in nothing. What came out of the conversation was that I still didn't learn a thing. I still don't really know how to be humble. This time, I believed in myself more.

I left the convent on the night of 3 January 1993. I chose to leave that night not knowing the fate of my life outside the convent. I was the first of the six to leave. Just a few months and years later, my brothers and sisters left the convent for various reasons. Many preferred to continue their college education and study in their chosen courses. Others followed, leaving for months in a row and reportedly had a relationship with each other and eventually become husband and wife. There were also those who married their classmates in college or ended up with their childhood friends. I haven't heard from anyone else.

It was November 2008. After sixteen years, I found myself in front of the Holy Eucharist Church again, our convent. I was invited to be the groomsman of a former brother whom I had lived with and became close to me. He chose the convent to hold his wedding because it was the venue of their romance with his fiancée whom he had met there as a member of the church choir.

Everything came back to me. I once again smelled in my mind and heart the incense, candles, fireworks, the breviary, the perfume of the saints and the host when I was inside the convent church. I was sent back to the convent that I never thought would happen again. Because when I left it that night of 1993, I really thought my life would be in vain because I would return again to the hardships of life outside of it.

But the convent taught me something so that I wouldn't get lost. It taught me to always have God as refuge in all my thoughts and hopes as a human being. Many more trials came into my life but I overcame them all because my spiritual foundation was deepened within the convent. And because of this foundation, to this day, I still continue to believe and follow myself.

Service Crew

I learnt the most startling truth of life the moment I left the convent: I had to work hard on my own if I want to graduate. I lost my scholarship that came with being a religious brother. So to speak, I began working and supporting myself. After failing to be a brother for almost a year, I would become part of the working student population in this country. But I wasn't hired that fast. My resilience would be tested first by the challenges of being a rejected applicant.

Job seekers in the Philippines face a lot of problems. Well, I found myself needing money at the time when I was applying for work—from buying a sheet of biodata (résumé writing wasn't very popular back then), borrowing fares, borrowing neat clothes from friends for interviews to being absent from class because of job hunting. I was able to survive these trials even though my daily struggles were intense. However, the true problem I faced was my lack of confidence. I felt weak in that aspect. My strength back then? It was my inferiority complex.

I was always stuttering at interviews. Often, when the interviewer spoke fast, my mind would slow down and I couldn't answer right away. My face would look serious. By the end of the interview, after a few failed attempts, I discovered the pattern of questioning followed by interviewers at the companies I wanted to join. Soon, I would find the courage to answer with confidence. I just got tired of failure and left no room for shame.

Let it be. Also, there were long queues of applicants of which I was a part. This was the queue of applicants who wanted to work as service crew member in many of the country's large fast food chains. Companies like these always hired part-time students, so I tried my luck in getting hired.

Even though I was confident of my answers in the interview, no one hired me. I began wondering. Was my expression too sour? People who ate their food won't throw up if the first thing they saw was my face as they entered the restaurant! So I also learnt how to smile. In fact, I changed my serious-face tactic in the interview with an 'untiring smile of a beauty queen' during the interview. But with the number of applications I did before, whether it was for a company or a franchise store, it still didn't work. I passed the exams but failed the interview. Sometimes, at the first interview, they would promise, 'we'll call you'. But there wasn't any call back.

I even had the experience of using a manager to back up my application. When I got to the final interview, he stapled my recommendation letters addressed to the branch manager. I slept over it for two nights. I didn't even try to secretly open the letter. I didn't want them to notice that I opened it and be caught. I was confident that it was acceptable because there was already a recommendation paper. But the truth is, there were so many stapled letters because he never told me that the recommendation was actually a rejection letter. I only found out after queuing up for a long time and was told 'we'll call you' again.

My soul was broken that day. It hurt pretty bad! I had been applying for two years and the self-confidence was fading away. Fortunately, one of my dentist friends noticed my ugly teeth. He fixed it for free by putting a jacket on them. It was here that I realized my broken, non-white and saw-like teeth, which I had taken care of when I was still in high school, were the culprit!

Who would want to eat in a restaurant where the service crew smiled like their teeth was 'chainsaw massacred'!

It was 1995 when I solved the problem of my ugly smile. Finally, I was accepted and became a full service crew at Colonel Harland Sanders, a fried chicken restaurant. It was my first year as a transferee at the Philippine Normal University (PNU), and I decided to become a student of teaching.

My schedule was at the opening hour from morning to noon. Four hours a day. Twenty-one pesos per hour back then. From seven to eleven o'clock in the morning. But it wasn't religiously followed because the peak hours were from eleven to noon when there are a lot of people eating in that area on Makati Avenue. I would often leave the store at one in the afternoon. My duty ran for five to six hours. Then, I'd quickly catch a ride on a jeep and a bus to go to the evening school at PNU. It was so common for me to look sluggish and sleepy among my classmates and professors during classes. But eventually, I got used to it and was alert and active in class even when tired.

I know that I am a hardworking person because I have become ripped from doing household chores since my childhood days in the province. However, in my first few days at the store, because I didn't even know the exact work to be done and I was still an observer, I did nothing but wipe, wash a little, and lift the cooking utensils. I moved slowly. For my first line of tasks, I was immediately assigned to the kitchen. The seniors began talking about me. They said I was *petiks*—the slang for lazy. After all, they were assigned to coat the chicken with all-purpose flour, fry the chicken, rub the burnt cooking oil on the pans, peel, crush and mix the potatoes. And since I hadn't met anyone or been acquainted with them, I could sometimes hear them allude to me during their banters. 'Hey! Lazy boy move!' or 'That thing you've been wiping there's going to be shiny!' I chose not to answer back. I don't want to be a sore loser and

I told myself, just let them wait. When I'm ready, these petty fools will chase me.

And that day came. Suddenly. In fact, quick. As fast as I could walk around the kitchen and memorize the processes from preparation to cooking. It even got to the point where I was doing their tasks when I felt they were slower. From being lazy, they called me *hussle*, which means fast worker. I eventually became friends with those who had once been my bullies. The truth is I got to know and be friends with all the service crew not only because of my speed at work. It was the day when we were able to tease each other and invite one another to drink during occasions. Outside work, I was their listener and spokesperson for their grievances to those in administration whenever there was a meeting in the store. They knew that my course was social science. They said that I was good at arguments because I went with the flow. The managers saw me as an activist, but it didn't have a negative meaning for them since many of them were almost the same age as me and some of us had become close friends. We went out to drink at times after a busy evening schedule.

Like the experiences that any worker can gain in any factory, my work was more meaningful and colourful as I eventually knew the culture attached to being a service crew.

When I started having classes in the morning, the store manager assigned me to the closing schedule. I would be in from six in the afternoon until eleven in the evening. In fact, the store closed exactly at nine o'clock. We spent the last two hours calculating the revenue, and disposing and cleaning the cooking utensils and the entire store.

Evening was the busiest time of the day. We scraped off all the oil that had dried on the stoves. Then, soak the cooking utensils to soften the dry and hard chicken skins that clung to the trays. The kitchen, pantry and dining area floors were swept, wetted and washed with soap. Then, they were mopped. Even the walls were wiped first with a soapy rag and followed by a dry rag. The mirrors must also be shiny and clear before the store was closed, so further soaping and wiping was done on them. We stacked up the tables in one corner and placed the chairs on top of them. All corners, up to the comfort room should be clean. Also, the flour, chicken, vegetables and other condiments had to be arranged in the storage and some parts must be ready so that the service crews who opened the store in the morning could start quickly. This was called endorsement. Every night, at each closing time, we had specific tasks depending on which station we were assigned. Kitchen, pantry, dining station, I worked in all of them. Later on, because I taught myself this job, I also worked at other fast food chains in the country. But I was always assigned most of the time in the dining area, especially when I became a service crew at a cheap pizza shop where the branches grew and multiplied because the company bought the red 'sexless bee'. The managers assigned beautiful crew members in the dining area for they had beautiful smiles and looks. Well, that's it!

It was fun but I still wanted to work in the kitchen because I was always left hungry when I was assigned to the dining area. Especially the 'hunger for respect' from the many customers that think they bought you if they can order things that they can do themselves. I often heard the calls 'Hey!', 'Sssst!', and 'Boy!' followed by their orders. I felt degraded so I always asked myself what was the use of our nameplates facing them? Why can't we be called by our names? Are they too hungry and their eyes blurred to read our names or are their ego too full and want to behave like the 'bourgeoisie' because they paid so much for their food? But of course, these complaints and grievances were kept inside ourselves simply because 'the customer is always right'.

So I looked forward to being assigned again to the kitchen because the kitchen has many 'blessings'. In the first store

I worked in, I would live by eating chicken butt and by drinking Michael Jordan and Olajuwon every morning.

It's so disgusting to eat chicken butt. For as long as I can remember, I've always been eating fried chicken and I avoided it. Once when I tried tasting it, I was struck by its slimy poultry taste and how it juiced inside my mouth. And I was thinking about what came out of it when it was alive. Think about its real function whether in a chicken or a person. I would back out whenever somebody served it. But one morning, I would suddenly wake up craving for the taste of chicken butt and soon, I would search for it every morning when my schedule is at the opening and make it my breakfast. So when I opened the store, I would request the manager to assign me to the kitchen.

I learnt that it was simple to fry chicken. First, bread the chicken parts into special flour—the corporate secret is the herbs and spices they mix in it—using a specific number of mixes. This was followed by specifically placing the chicken parts on each floor of a bird-cage-like container that was divided in the middle and made of steel. The 'cage' was immersed in an oil-filled deep frying cooker that is also made of steel and powered by a mixture of LPG and electricity. Then, it was covered tightly. In just fifteen minutes, the chicken was done and its smell wafted in the air—aromatic, crunchy, and extremely tender inside. It was shiny with oil. The third step was to drip the oil for about five minutes. Then, open the 'cage' and transfer the identical parts of the chicken to the trays one by one following a specific arrangement.

In the third step, we ate the chicken butt.

As the lard dripped, we would sometimes look at the thigh part of the chicken and find a very large butt. And when the desired butt was found, we would use the tongs to handle the chicken and quickly squeeze and tear it apart. It must be obviously torn. The said part should still look like a butt.

Then we would stuff the accumulated buttocks in the pandesals. When the pandesal was gone, one by one we simply went inside the walk-in chiller—the store's refrigerator that housed almost all the raw food and can accommodate at least five people. Here we took Michael Jordan (mango juice) and Olajuwon (orange juice). We would swallow gallons of it without mixed water and feel its thick syrup flush inside our throats. When we came out, we quickly gulped tap water. I was full! We mastered this art of stealing chicken butts from one of the earliest Jedi in the kitchen.

It happened once that I was caught. I didn't realize that our security guard was behind me. In such a job, being late means being fired at once. Nervously, I offered a portion of my chicken butt to the guard. To the surprise of my companions, the guard, smiling, reached for his part of the ass and then swallowed it. Oh man, he was hungry too. When he left, my companions sang the chorus of 'Himala', meaning miracle, by the band River Maya while laughing and beating me on different parts of the body. I felt like I graduated from cursillo that morning.

Our lunch depended on the allotted time of our thirty-minute break. We went on a break in batches. So we had different companions at lunch. The food was best at the first store I worked at because you could choose a portion of chicken from the store. In other stores I entered, we had to contribute to buy our lunch outside the store. Of course, we chose the largest portion of the chicken. But one cup of rice wasn't enough. With our heavy workload, I took this job so I could eat free food.

Where else to hustle but to 'steal' food again. Before leaving the kitchen, we wrapped the spare rice in 'plastic blur' which is of course illegal. It would be simply be tucked into our boots and under the heel. The rice was hot so we simply tiptoed as we went to the dining area.

One day, the problem came when I was only halfway to the table, the guard suddenly stopped me. He asked who won the basketball game last night. The story lasted about five minutes and my foot got tired from tiptoeing. Some co-workers who were already at the table saw it. The 'fellow-thieves' were silently laughing. I got to the table and caressed my burnt heel while biting into my food and my fellow rice thieves kept on laughing and relentlessly rubbing my back.

Other students saw the work of a service crew as a status symbol. Back then, it was like owning a new iPhone today. That you'd rather buy an iPhone first than spend it on food. Even though we didn't earn that much, many of us looked forward to our payday not just to meet the needs at school or at home, but to keep up with the hobbies of our well-off peers. Some spent it for a gimmick at night. Splurge on alcohol. Waste on a romantic date. Or in a night at the motel. So between work, it was common to hear stories about getting drunk and dancing in popular bars or in the houses of our colleagues. They'd invite anyone who would eat out and go to the movies. And who among the female co-workers got 'laid' in Uncle Telmo's house. After pay day, it was also common for somebody to come in with a strong hangover, irritable and almost exhausted, finish a gallon of Michael Jordan and Olajuwon and purge the alcohol with chicken butt. Some managers also knew this because some of them, I would say, joined in these trips. A few days later, you would hear many of them borrowing money because their daily budgets had depleted.

I'll admit, although not always like other co-workers, there have been a few times that I experienced them as well. But only as far as drinking and borrowing money. I almost 'got laid' because that time I was working, and I got Joida pregnant. And she would give birth to our first-born, Kala. Then I juggled building a family, studying in college, and working fulltime.

Although there were some successful romance stories that developed between co-workers, it was also common among service crew persons to be in third parties. I have friends who had a romantic relationship at work but after work, they would go their separate ways to their original boyfriends and girlfriends. There were braver ones who would even introduce their 'sweetheart at work' as 'my co-worker!' to their significant other waiting at home.

The painful thing was that at times it was not just a boyfriend or girlfriend waiting but a wife. In one of the food chains I worked for, I found out that some co-workers were in a relationship and had slept with the manager. I avoided dating at work because it was too heavy for me juggling between being a father and being a college student. My conscience weighed heavily over my decisions especially since my firstborn was a girl. But that didn't mean I was never tempted.

At the pizza store where I worked at the Ayala Terminal, there was a service crew who was a friend of my female manager. She worked in another branch but on some days, especially on her day off, she would hang out at our store pretending to visit her manager friend. I later find out—also from her—that she went there to see me.

One night, my manager set me up with her. She insisted on inviting me, along with the others, after the store closed to the house where she was staying in Pasay. She said we would have a few drinks. That time I didn't know she had a motive so I naively joined. We were enjoying drinks and I later found out that I was so drunk I couldn't go home. I would also find out that the others had left and that only about three pairs of us remained in the party. She escorted me to her room on the second floor of the house. While walking upstairs, she whispered to my ears that I was the reason she always came to our branch.

She has fallen in love with me since a long time. I answered her with mumbled words and a drunken smile.

At the bed, she laid me down neatly then turned off the lights and nodded. She started kissing me on the cheek towards the back of the ear to the lips. I'm not a rock so I kissed her back. She caressed me and I caressed her back. She gently rubbed my pants and I gently rubbed her back. Then, she groped inside my pants and I did it to her as well. And like a flash of lightning, I woke up to my senses. Even though I was drunk, I knew the smell and the feeling on my finger. It was slimy and rough. She didn't know she had a period.

Menstruation got rid of my drunkenness. She suddenly got up and quickly ran inside the bathroom, and only came out when she thought I was asleep. She turned her back to me. I knew she was very embarrassed. The next morning, while she was still sound asleep, I left without a note. But for a moment I was stunned because I saw my name on her wall. They were cut-outs in different designs, and they were also written with different coloured permanent markers on the wallpaper itself.

I could no longer remember exactly how I felt. Like pity with a mix of sadness. Also a lack of sleep and a headache. I went downstairs to see two pairs of my co-workers still hugging in their sleep on the floor and the sofa. All the evidence of our drinking night was scattered everywhere. I hurried out and on the way home, made up a reason as to why I came home in the morning.

But she couldn't stop visiting me at the store. I deliberately avoided her even though I felt like she was always looking at me. Inside me, there was regret. Regret of the missed chance. Regret of my situation. But because the face of my eldest baby girl was more powerful in my mind, I restrained myself from engaging with her before I could even fall in love. I felt sorry for her, especially whenever I thought of how she was endlessly writing and cutting my name on the wall of her room.

Not to be proud of this but I became the leader among the service crews I worked with in all the stores I've been to. So even with those in administration, I felt a sense of mutual respect and camaraderie. One night, my female manager, who had been closest to me as a friend, asked me not to go home yet. When everyone had left and there were only the two of us inside and the light was off, she suddenly burst into tears. She confessed to me that she had been in a relationship with a married man for several years. She said that she could no longer continue the relationship due to many complications and that she felt very hurt by this.

I just listened to her tell her stories of pain. I knew that having somebody listen to her was all she needed that night. When she calmed down, I accompanied her to the jeepney terminal, and I waited for the jeepney to disappear from my sight before going home. I haven't seen her since. That was my last night as a service crew because I was done.

I missed a few days before the end of my contract at every store I worked for. There is a tradition that when you are 'endo', or end of contract, you expect your colleagues to splash you with cold water filled with ice, as a farewell symbol. Someone will hug you. Then some will kiss you goodbye. Some will cry, especially the women. And there will also be promises to meet soon and visit, even though we know that it would never happen again.

I left early not because I was avoiding the ice bucket farewell party. To be frank, it felt good to get wet. I left because I want to avoid the sadness of separation. No matter how good the fellowship is, everyone will still feel sad to be separated. It would have been better for me to run away because I would be sadder to formally say goodbye and leave.

I remember working as a service crew for six fast food stores of four different sister companies when I was still in college. Each contract lasted six months. I laugh at it now when I remember that I didn't even process my backpay because of laziness. The companies were lucky then to hire me. They saved up on salary! But I know that more than backpay, my foundation as a worker today is more deeply rooted in my experiences as a service crew. Of course, I had to let go of my negative traits. It was still with me when I was young. So I was luckier. In the most recent company I joined as a service crew, more obligations would add up as a father. Kala was only a year old when Joida became pregnant with my son Rebo. I had to focus more on the rest of my studies, and I looked forward to more permanent and professional employment for my children's future.

On some days when I get to visit a fast food restaurant, I strike a smile when I see the quick students working as a service crew. I also can't help but look back and think. I realize that the experiences and struggles of working as service crew are not far removed from other kinds of workers. Even though they say they are younger and have only their own ways of leisure. What happens at work also gives them problems and lets them grow. Just like me who until now is still disgusted with eating chicken butts.

So every time I eat at a fast food chain, I make sure I'm not a complicated customer so I wouldn't have to add more to their problems. And I make sure that whenever I ask for help from them, I use their names so they know I respect them. Well, ask Michael Jordan and Olajuwon. They'll tell you all about it.

Baclaran

Back then, I knew the streetways of Baclaran very well. It was because I took jeepney rides to the far-flung villages of Niog in Cavite way back in high school. During my bus rides, as soon as I crossed the Magallanes Bridge from Makati, the scenery changed to the cityscapes of Pasay. And the city's mood comes off differently to me. The traffic on the side of Tramo Street appeared as crowded, polluted, and definitely bottle-necked. As one arrived at the jeepney bay of Baclaran, it became more crowded and hazy. There, I took a jeep to Niog. I really only saw the outer layers of Baclaran, the streets on its main thoroughfares. I entered its neighbourhoods when something discouraging happened to me and I had to take refuge in the Convent of the Four Nuns of Baclaran.

It was the year 2002 when the mother of my two children and I separated. We disagreed on a lot of things and so we decided to go our separate ways. I remember it was night, and we could no longer hear each other's voices because we shouted and blamed each other. In the background, the cries of my little ones erupted. I was done with it. Like a bursting volcano, the lava of our pent-up anger exploded. This happened more than once. And any restraint we had for each other was just for the kids. This relationship was done and so, that night, I chose to walk out the door of the small room we were renting carrying a rattan bag with my clothes and teaching aids that I quickly gathered. I made it for the kids. I didn't want them to grow up always watching us fight. I believe it's not enough to be together if nothing came out of that relationship. It was like a tree decaying from termites, inside out. My children who will weave their character and dreams in the future will not be able to stand us fighting every time.

I left that night not knowing where to go. Fortunately, cell phones had become popular and I had made new friends.

I was in my second year of teaching when I entered a small private school in Bayani Road inside Fort Bonifacio. The Libingan ng mga Bayani (The Cemetery of Heroes) was walking distance from the school. Surrounding it were the new subdivisions of military officers. In fact, almost all my students here were children of military families. Here, I met the Maths teacher, Mr Edward. If the area is surrounded by macho military men, Teacher Edward was the gentle teacher of the children of these macho military men. I didn't have a problem with that. I befriended him as long as I felt he was a real person. I also made many friends like Edward who I knew were closet gays, especially in front of students. 'Intellectual gay men', as they said.

When I asked him where he lived, he always said that he was a tenant on Airport Road in Baclaran, living with three friends. He also once mentioned that there was a vacant bed in their rented room. This information encouraged me to head to Baclaran on the night of my separation after texting Edward to pick me up outside the church.

It was about eleven o'clock in the evening when I got out of the church. Just a few minutes later, Edward arrived, who I saw for first time dressed in thin, tight shorts and a t-shirt. Here he is! I saw the real Edward come out, I told myself. But I was wrong. It was not true yet. There was something even more real that almost pushed me back to the house I had left.

That night, I walked inside the neighbourhoods of Baclaran for the first time. Airport Road was far from the church for the new arrivals like me. I had already texted Edward the complete reason of my asking for his help; he told me not to worry because he had mentioned my arrival to the landlord and that I would become an extra tenant right away. He told me the steward was very kind because they considered her an elder sister. Her name was Kulot. I wondered if Sister Kulot was an old woman. The flirt laughed out loud. Sister Kulot—for whom I was very anxious—and Niño and Alice who were with her in the room—which was now bothered and stressed me out— were gay. And he told me, I shouldn't call him Edward when he came home because his name is Dianne in Baclaran! This is where the fear exploded in my heart. The pain, anger, and confusion that I felt that night were overwhelming. I wanted to back out and to Joida. But I was defeated and felt ashamed of the kindness of Edward a.k.a. Dianne. I was scared to think that avoiding a fierce fight in Makati would only result in swarms of people 'attacking' me in Baclaran!

The rented rooms were on the second floor. The house was found at the second alley from a convenience store that is the landmark of the Airport Road if you are already inside Baclaran. The second floor was small but fitted three bedrooms. The gay landlord Kulot lived alone in the first room and the other three—Edward, Niño, and Alice—were together on two double-decker beds in the second room. The third room was for Kulot's three young nephews who helped him in the grilling and selling of barbecue. There was a folding table and sink in the area that also served as the living room. The window on the side of the sink was empty. The Airport Road was seen from the window, especially the beer houses lining up on the streets. Everything was made of wood. The whole house was old. Cleanliness and order freaks wouldn't have been able to last a day. But for someone like me who was desperate for help and needed to sleep that night, this was paradise. After all, until Edward and I arrived and I was formally introduced to his housemates, my fear of being 'attacked' by gay men hadn't ended. Fortunately, I was so tired that evening from everything that happened to me that I fell asleep. But it wasn't going to be that way for long.

I was ashamed of myself for what I had thought of them the first night I stayed there. Even though I had only just met them, they considered me a long-time friend. The nights I was afraid that one of them might crawl into my bed or touch me while I slept. But that did not happen. Or even flirt with me. I scolded myself for judging them so quickly. Because every day and night we met after each other's work, they lent me their ears and became my cheerleaders especially on the nights I could not sleep due to so much sadness and crying because I sorely missed my children. The four pointed out that whatever inner conflicts I felt that time could be relieved by a shot of gin-pomelo.

Sister Kulot—*kulot* is the word for curly and her long hair is really curly—was mother superior. She owned a barbecue business and was patronized by travellers to and from Baclaran. It was common for the house to smell of the boiled innards of pork and chicken before dawn. The sisters also had different sources of income. Edward was a teacher like me. Niño was an insurance agent, and Alice was a beautician in a parlour in Baclaran. Whenever somebody among us got pay check, we could expect to have a drink before bed every night. Especially at the nights when they felt my intense pain—even though I often hid in the room to cry—I could expect someone to buy gin and pomelo-flavoured juice right away, which was to be our fuel for a long night of storytelling and opening up (I will clarify, opening up my inner self). We picked up Kulot's leftovers from her business—if there was excess—or bought chips from the sari-sari store. It was at these moments that I got to know them very well.

Kulot came from the Quezon province and ended up in Manila just like others who wanted to venture into the city. She met the landlord who, after deciding to move out, entrusted her with the rental business. And in order to survive, she went into the business of grilling entrails. Edward was her first tenant. Then came Alice. Edward took his friend Niño with him one day to that place, and he too became a tenant there. When I arrived, I named them the Four Nuns in the Convent of Baclaran. They loved it and in return, named me their Priest of the Convent.

There came a time when I would constantly remind them to cool their heads when they secretly fought in the heat of drinking. They stopped because Father gave a homily. After an evening of drinking, often the only problem left for us was waking up in the morning once the hangover kicked in because of the 'mass' last night and the clogged toilets. Apart from these, I only remember the funny stories they shared at night like their private gay adventures.

Edward, who came out as bisexual had a relationship with a man and a woman. The man, he said, was gayer than him. This guy often gave him an allowance that he used for his date nights with the woman. I asked him if he wasn't afraid of getting an STD since he also had a sexual relationship with the two. He told me he was careful. I was silent after that and thought about the exchange of saliva and other bodily liquids during sex. I can't quite imagine how not even one of them got sick even though he said he was careful. Of course, I just kept it to myself.

Kulot met the man she loved in Baclaran. This man came from the provinces and when he decided to go abroad, Kulot paid for all the paperwork up to the placement fee. He did it for their future. Once the guy left for abroad, the man broke up with her. Kulot didn't know anymore what happened to her lover or talk to him, so she could get back some of the money she spent on him. After that, she decided never to love again. Of the four of them, Kulot was the one you could talk to without the flamboyance of a gay man. She was serious in life. A true mother.

Niño was the hopeless romantic. He said he had a crush on a male co-worker. He would often give gifts of things to be noticed but it had no effect so he thought of another way to get closer to him. He'd sometimes join him for lunch. He would go out with his colleague as long as his crush was also included. He even became his stalker! Once, he followed him in a taxi until he reached home. There he found out that he had a live-in partner waiting for him. It was very painful for Niño but he told himself not to give up. He was right because his crush wasn't married yet. He said he would not give up and try and snatch the man from his relationship. And 'promise Ferdie, I will succeed!' he declared to me while wetting his lips to which the three queers would reply, 'Plangak, Precisely!'

Alice was the most flirtatious when it came to men. Even if it was a high school boy or somebody older than her, she would accompany them as long as she saw them waiting outside the parlour where she worked. She would get excited if the man winked back at her. So it was expected that Alice would always borrow money from the three queers. But sometimes someone would treat her to something. She even told us when she was given money.

But the payoff was intense. She was allegedly mistaken for a woman by a drunk soldier at a beer house on Airport Road. He allegedly invited her out. Even though she had diarrhoea that night, Sister Alice didn't miss the opportunity. But when they were inside the taxi, she confessed that she was not a woman. Because he was drunk, the soldier seemed okay about it. She even received five hundred pesos but the soldier directed the taxi not to the motel but to the Cemetery of Heroes! And in a crowded and hidden corner of the tomb, and without a word, the soldier pulled down his pants. And he quickly fucked her. Fortunately, she was no longer a virgin. He was able to withstand the pump of the soldier boy. Sadly, it smelt! It seems that the drunken soldier woke up to his senses and the weapon of mass destruction was quickly pulled out. And that was when the soldier suddenly went crazy and beat the hell out of Sister Alice because apart from the smell, there was peanut butter clinging to the 'weapon' of the 'brave' soldier!

Alice went home with nothing but bruises on her face and body, crying while the three queers laughed. She said it was a good thing that she was paid to buy medicine for the bruises. My stomach ached with laughter when she told this story. It was one of those nights that I forgot the pain of the situation that brought me to that place. I also learnt to laugh at the pain and tiredness I was feeling. The strong sense of humour of the four was a big help. Well, it didn't last for long. There were times when I couldn't avoid being alone.

During the day, almost all of us were outside working, but there were days when I come home early after teaching. I was alone at times like this. Then I did the laundry in a cramped bathroom. If you looked at it, sometimes you could see something floating in the toilet. I had to stomach what I saw and right away clean it before I washed my clothes. While doing this, I'd silently swear at the anonymous culprit of the floating evidence that did not even give a fuck to flush its resentment. I would hang the clothes outside the third bedroom window with the wire hangers. The clotheslines were too short and often someone had already hung up their clothes. So I just washed a little bit and prioritized the uniforms I use at work.

There were times I would just catch myself crying while doing laundry in the bathroom. I would pause from scrubbing my clothes because the thought of my children would sometimes visit me in these quiet times. My mind would wander, and sometimes I would think of giving up this separation and go back to them. But in less than a month, I knew that I would never go back because my brother Mike texted me that my children had left the house we were renting. Their mother brought my children to an exclusive home at a subdivision in Parañaque, which was owned by her older brother who also happened to work as a gay overseas Filipino worker in Japan.

Sometimes, after doing laundry or doing nothing, I would avoid staring into the blankness of the room. I was often stunned. If I wanted to fall asleep, I couldn't. A lot of worries entered my mind especially thinking about what would happen to me and my children. I had a habit of always being afraid of my future when everything was so uncertain for me. I would then pull myself up and leave the house to walk around the streets of Baclaran. Sometimes I'll hang out at Kulot's grill and have a chit chat when she was no longer busy selling. I also had the courage to walk the streets and alleys of the area with no definite plan of where to actually go. I just looked at the houses, the different kinds of people that lived in them and everything they did on every street I walked by. Luckily, no one pranked me. After all, Baclaran is everyone's pathway. I think there are more strangers here than acquaintances.

There were also days when I saved money for fare and walked the inbound road from Pasay Rotonda to the Airport Road along with the crowds shopping in Baclaran at night. I was literally dragged by the women working in the beer houses I passed by. It's a good thing I would free myself from their grasp. They did this to all men who passed by, especially those who were dressed for work. They would really shout to invite me to their beer house.

I saved money to eat food at a tapsilog—tapas, eggs, and fried rice—restaurant because I knew no one would leave food for me in the rented house. We also had our own ways of putting food on the table except on days when one of us had extra money or was in a generous mood and suddenly cooked a dish for everyone. Here I also discovered that I can cook. One day when I got home early, Kulot asked me to cook the galunggong that she bought because they would spend the night selling at the barbecue. I should cook it as sarciado. I don't know how to cook, I said. She told me it was easy. Before she left me, she taught me how to sauté the garlic and onions, to crush tomatoes and mix the eggs. All this was to be done after the galunggong had been fried and toasted. Then, I would put the fish sauce which I poured based on the saltiness I wanted. Come what may, I told myself.

I cooked the sarciadong galunggong. They enjoyed the dish and finished it up. Kulot said I was a fast learner and requested me to try cooking other dishes. She told me I had a good sense of taste. In fact, nothing was left on the plate after dinner. It was one of the nights we had a happy time inside the apartment. We drank more gin-pomelo after we were full. Then told stories until dawn. So I didn't expect that it would be followed by nights when their friendship fell apart.

Some nights I would be left in the room while planning a lesson in class. The young queers, on the other hand, would leave one by one to flirt or go on a date outside. The four nuns would leave the convent and go outside the church. Often, it was between eleven and midnight. They would simultaneously look for a booking—a man they'd like to get laid with. And the 'blessings from heaven' were said to be outside the Baclaran church. On nights when they were successful in searching for men, they would not bring home their found blessings. I don't know where they do the 'bookings'. I already knew what was going on. They did this often, every Saturday and Sunday night. But the nights came when I noticed that some of them would not go and would part ways. Until I noticed that our late nights of gin-pomelo had become less frequent till they stopped entirely. Their previous secret disputes also matured.

I started to hear from Edward about his irritation at what Alice was doing. He told me that she had become too flirty even though she had no money. Her debts added up. I also heard that Kulot charged Alice several times about a few months when she skipped on her share in the rent of the house. I indirectly heard their conversation inside Kulot's room. The house was too small for us and our rooms were only divided with plywood. Even if one didn't intend to listen, one could hear their voices annoyed at each other.

I came home one night and saw the four of them inside as if they were blind to each other. No one spoke a word. Suddenly they were all busy with what they were doing. When I simply asked the young queers why the house was so quiet, they said the four of them had just finished a shouting match.

I was not there to see how the fight began or how the blame rang out. All I know is, I arrived that evening with an air of anger and coldness inside the house. I could not be silenced. I memorized such situations, and I knew very well where this was headed based on what I had just experienced myself.

They may have chosen to fight at a time when they knew I wasn't coming yet. Or maybe it was just a coincidence. What I'm pretty sure of, is that they knew I wouldn't be able to intervene because that's what I do and even though they have known me even for a short time. I didn't want to add to the problem so I mediated in the affairs to fix what was broken.

One day I was surprised that Alice's pillows were no longer on her bed. Her clothes were no longer in the closet. When I looked for her that night with Niño, it confirmed my suspicion. Alice had moved out of the apartment. She left on her own. Then Niño admitted that he was also talking to a new landlord so he could move out. He said Edward and Kulot allegedly cut their communications with Alice and him. It was because the two wanted to move out and did not want them to be included. He also told me to get ready before they would ask me to leave as well. But I couldn't wait for them anymore to talk to me. I made the first move.

Kulot was very honest with me. She admitted that she planned to leave the house. She also said that they could no longer get along with the owner. And she also said that she didn't want to be with Alice and Niño anymore. She could no longer handle the behaviour of the two, especially since they acted like children who were always delayed on the rent. Edward, on the other hand, decided to go wherever Kulot would go. It would also be in Baclaran, a place that is a little far from the Airport Road. The two had been really close and have been friends for a long time so I expected it. But what I did not expect was their invitation to include me as well. At this point, I couldn't answer right away. I will think about it, I said. And I really thought about it.

It also took me two months more before I finally left Baclaran. It was short but it was heavy and deep. It was heavy because from the very beginning, this is how I felt the night I got there. I experienced being with someone when I was alone. It was deep because I experienced great sadness and anxiety, got stomach aches from long nights of laughter, met new extraordinary friends, and most of all, went through an intense reflection to better know myself and plan the paths ahead in the future. I just didn't think the ending would be this dramatic because I came from separation; I would also leave from a separation.

I decided not to go with Kulot and Edward. I thanked them for all their help and bid farewell a few days before they moved out. I know, even if they didn't say it, they were also sad when I left. I couldn't be with them anymore even though I knew I still wanted to be with them. I felt like even if that happened, something would be missing. And I could no longer afford to experience another thing lacking in my life.

It was also that night when I left Baclaran. I said goodbye to them in the morning so I didn't have to wait for them when I left. Again, carrying the rattan bag and a few other personal stuff I had bought, I headed to a place that no one knew, far away from Baclaran. Even though I knew I was still not strong as a person, I prepared myself to accept loneliness.

There are separations that numb the soul. There are divorces that break the soul. There are others where you are left grateful because it happened. There are those that leave us angry forever, and there are those that come with forgiveness. When I was separated from my children, I felt the sharpest pain in my heart. It was the same when I was separated from the 'Four Nuns' in the 'Convent of Baclaran.' The pain seems to squeeze my heart. Even gin-pomelo couldn't drown the pain.

Six Saturdays of Beyblade

Beyblade, lots of Beyblades. One spins on the floor. Then, it becomes two. Later, it's five. All are colourful. Red, white, blue, green, silver, gold, yellow—a flurry of difference. Either plastic or steel, we'd buy lots of them every Saturday.

We always did this whenever my son Rebo and I met. I was sure he'd ask me to buy a new Beyblade, that's why I saved up for him. It's roughly 30 to 50 pesos or more depending on its design, energy layers, forge discs, and performance tips. I'd be lifting weights because I was sure Rebo would like me to carry him whenever we'd visit his favourite store at our barangay's local market.

The toy store's half a kilometre away from my mother's house where we would see each other often every Saturday. Rebo asks me to drop him down when we're both in front of the store so he can point to his favourite toy. As we approach, the seller welcomes us with a smile. He's known us for a long time, even the schedule of our visits. He's ready to pitch in the newest Beyblade that Rebo might like to buy. Rebo always looks first at the colours and design of the energy layers and the forge discs. Plastic or steel? That's just an afterthought. But for a long time now, Rebo chooses the plastic ones. He plays with the Beyblades way more than the other toys, like trucks and cars. Maybe because they're so much smaller. And unlike the latter, Beyblades can be carried anywhere: just pull them out of your pockets.

I was sure Rebo would pull out lots from his pockets. While he's getting ready for a 'battle,' I'd sometimes check my pockets and only feel my hands, remembering that I gave everything to him. The game is a contest of endurance, spinning longer than the opponent inside a plastic bucket called the Bey Stadium. If the opponent's Beyblade flies out of the ring, they lose. If the opponent's Beyblade stops spinning first, he loses. Yet, unlike the other kids who give up after a defeat, Rebo continues to fight. He'll grip the saw-like teeth of the ripcord harder than usual. He'll tighten the lock of the Beyblade launcher as if he's holding a gun. And when the game begins, he quickly pulls out the ripcord from the narrow hole, releasing the Beyblade like a flying saucer spinning down to the platform to fight again.

For four Saturdays, my youngest son fought battles with his Beyblades in the field of play. For eleven months, he fought leukaemia in the hospice of feelings.

* * *

To a teacher like me, April is summer break. To my youngest son who will be turning four years old, these are the days he'll play outside with his cousins.

It was the last week of March 2003 when he ran a fever for a week. When the fever broke, a few days passed and he lost his appetite. Then, he turned pale. By the first Saturday of April when I saw him again, he didn't want me to stop carrying him because he got tired quickly. Little by little, bruises appeared.

First, it was on the legs, then on the arms, until these patches spread like wildfire and were found on his foot, chest, and thighs. His lips paled as if soaked in vinegar. The clinic, a few blocks from here, came immediately to my mind. I would have liked to tell the doctor: 'I have 500 pesos here and I'll look for more if needed. Tell me what's happening to my son!' But even after the fees had reached 3,000—on top of pleas, donations, and debts, three doctors and two clinics—and after I had numbed myself against my son's screams every time a needle pricked him for a blood test, the illness remained without a name. His heart rate was high for his age, his red blood count plummeting—these were the doctors' only interpretations. Failure to diagnose. This case needs more tests. More blood tests and pain. The muscle aches and shivers. Me, my wife, and our family got numb hearing more of these words each day.

The failed attempts at diagnosis were difficult to bear. I had to endure not only the pain in my knees but also the weight I carried in my chest as I stood here waiting in the hospital. Whatever the results were, I must be ready. Rebo's mother stood in long snake-like lines at the largest public hospital in the country. They were lining up for a hospital card to schedule a consultation with a paediatrician who specialized in diagnosing the symptoms.

That day, Rebo wanted me to carry him, not his mother. This is what he wanted: Even if his Naynay[1] could carry him, what he wanted was for his Taytay to carry him and hold his Ate[2] Kala in my other hand.

'Because it's Saturday, Saturday should not end yet. Taytay should not leave early because I will have to wait again for another Saturday or his pay day before I see him again. Never mind leaving Naynay for a few hours; she's with me every day. I just want Taytay to carry me, hold me, tell me a story, play with me, buy "ays wis" [ice cream] and "babuygyam" [bubblegum] for me, and let me take a nap on his chest because it's just Saturday!'

---

[1] A term of endearment 'Tatay', which is Filipino for Daddy or Papa. Naynay is a word play for Nanay, which is Filipino for Mother or Mama.

[2] Ate is a Filipino word for an older sister.

I know these are the exact words he would want to say if he could let his young mind and his stuttering tongue to speak.

When Rebo got sick, a year and a half had passed since my separation from Joida. There were many disagreements. We looked in different directions. And money was often scarce: the result of a young and unripe marriage. I don't want to go anymore into the details of our separation. This is one of those memories I have buried deep in the mud. There came a point in my life when we had to forget the past and be civil for the children. This was when I was living on my own in a place no one must know about. Our kids lived in Joida's sister's house. That time, I had the opportunity to teach in a big and prestigious private school for rich kids, and I was able to withdraw liveable wages from the ATM. And unlike other fathers who leave their children with nothing after breaking up with their wives, I made sure that the larger part of my 'two-week's worth of wealth' went to my two children and what remained was saved up, just enough for me to drink a little beer.

* * *

It was painful to realize that the undying love I had for my children was not enough to shield them from a deadly attack.

Acute Lymphocytic Leukemia, also known as ALL, is a type of leukaemia common among children like Rebo. Chemotherapy is the only treatment. A series of cycles for the treatment takes weeks. Induction, consolidation, maintenance: three phases of treatment. Six, four, down to one strong dosage must enter my son's fragile body. These drugs will kill the cancer blasts that grow inside him. These drugs, blind to anything in their path, can destroy even the healthiest of organs and cause further complications.

We had been in the hospital for two weeks before the name of his disease was disclosed to us. We never left the hospital from the first day we took him for a check-up, hoping that the doctor would just prescribe drugs for anaemia or something else that would make his heartbeat normal again. The doctor's words were a deafening rush of details and interpretation. Yet I managed to somehow process it slowly, notwithstanding my benumbed mind. Rebo's face flashes before me: he is crying in pain everyday during blood tests and blood transfusions. The needles puncture his arms, his feet, his hips, his hands, and any other part where an unswollen vein appears. Blood flows freely in the tubes.

Rebo is a picture of many spots. Small and large bruises, red and dark rashes.

He is a picture of a balding child, losing his hair to chemotherapy.

He is a picture of many fallen hairs swept by the breeze, not knowing where the wind blows.

Radiation or genetics? We were uncertain. Simply put, his bones failed to develop and his marrow wasn't able to produce enough blood for a long and healthy life. His bones never grew.

Buto, dugo, pesteng buto! Pesteng dugo![3] No parent would ever want to hear what I heard. My son doesn't just have diarrhoea or fever. He is dying.

* * *

We stayed in the hospital for a long time. I thought it was a month, then it became two, then three, and then four, until

---

[3]   Peste is a Filipino swear word which means parasite. Buto is Filipino for bones. Dugo is Filipino for blood. In this context, I chose to keep the original swearing to keep the author's voice and intention.

I forgot how many months had passed. What I was sure of, though, was that we would stay longer.

'I graduated with a bachelor's in education but I can't find a job.'

'Actually, even if you teach right now, you can't handle it.'

'I agree, Sir.'

'Can't you afford a rent of 300 pesos a day?'

'Not really, Sir.'

'All right, show this form at the Social Services office. To your right.'

'Thank you, Sir! Thank you very much!'

I have to pretend and lie so Rebo can be transferred to the hospital's Charity Ward. At least here, Rebo can sleep on a mattress that is much more comfortable than the metal bed with wheels in the Emergency Room. Plus, there's a TV. If he's lucky to get the remote first, he can catch up on his favourite show. There are lots of other people watching too: the sick (from the severe cases to the critical), the relatives at each bedside (from the laughing ones to those crying or sleeping), and the visitors (from the hurried to the lingering). In this ward, illness manifests in all people from all walks of life. There are some who live in poor urban areas. Some come from the nearest to the farthest provinces. They hope to get well here. All of them are praying for donations to come from famous yet unnamed philanthropists who sometimes visit them because everyone's desperately in need, even for a cheap injection.

While the bed and food are free, we still have to buy all the prescription medicines and medical supplies needed for the cancer treatment. Even with my daily grind, I have to stay here to save money. Back then, I was earning fifteen thousand pesos a month, and if the Philippine General Hospital had found out, Rebo would have been removed from the charity ward. He would have had to be transferred to a costly private room.

I prayed hard for him to be allowed to stay in that place. My greatest expense was all of his medicines, which was around six to eight thousand pesos a week. That doesn't even include the injections, dextrose, tubes, the food that he craved, the laboratory fees outside the hospital for his blood analysis, or my fares. If you were previously bad at Maths, now you'd probably be the smartest because you'd do lots of accounting for all the cash that went in and out, letting out a deep sigh at the end of the day.

You would also learn to read strangers. The noisy and the quiet ones beside you, the generous and the parasitic. The mean and happy nurses. The snobbish and approachable doctors. The smart and stupid interns—especially those who pricked needles into my son eight times and still didn't draw any blood— they deserve my anger. The heartless laboratory technicians who didn't accept the amount of blood samples even though the doctor approved it. *What do you think you can do with my son's blood? Scoop it from a bucket?* And the relatives who were calm at first then lost their minds from depression. The sick are constantly noisy: either in bursts of laughter or wails of despair, both young and old. The quietest among them? Those intubated souls.

As for Rebo, once the ritual of taking his blood is over, he turns into this frolicsome, naughty kid. 'Remove this dextrose from me! I want to visit the other beds!'

Often, the people in the ward make fun of him. 'Go away, you're not sick, eh!'

He claps back with the bat of an eyelash, pulls out his tongue, and makes funny gestures. After a month, everybody knows '*Rebo bulol at kulit*'[4] in the Charity Ward.

* * *

---

[4] Bulol means tongue-tied and kulit means naughty.

Help poured from everywhere; even the smallest donation kept my son alive.

'Ma, has Tita Naida sent her remittance? How about Lola Conching?'

'Kapitan, thank you for the donation, ha!'

'Councilor, how do I go again to the Sweepstakes office? By the way, thank you for giving us the collections from the zone leaders. My mother cried in front of them.'

'Tita Marilyn, I'll just pay this when I get back on my feet.'

'What? These came from the donation drive of Tita Jean's students?'

'Tita Vic, please take care of Kala for now, ha! I can't leave Joida alone at the hospital, eh.'

'Kala, don't be naughty. Behave!'

'Bro, have you told the gang? Just a few pints of blood will be donated.'

'Thank you, compadres! Drinks on me next time. Just eat bitter gourd for now.'

'Ma'am, sir, I will be absent today. I need to be at the hospital. Thank you for the kind offering of the Faculty Club and the other departments.'

'Sure. You can pray for Rebo at the hospital. We'll wait for you there.'

We stayed at the hospital for five months until Rebo reached the last phase of treatment, the maintenance stage. It was September, which meant that he would visit the hospital once a month for his chemo. This would go on for three years. By then, Rebo had celebrated his fourth birthday and some hair had regrown on his scalp. I expected that my son would get well by the time he was seven, a ripe age for going back to school. I was sure that he wouldn't stammer anymore.

Outside, my son seemed like the healthy boy that he once was. Play over here, play over there. Eat here, eat there. Except when we returned to the hospital for a chemotherapy session. Each time a session ended, my son looked like a withered vegetable for three days. He didn't want to swallow anything except water. He didn't want to bite anything except an ice cube. *'An ini 'Tay nan aawan o!* [Tay, my body's so warm!]' He threw up a lot and felt irritated all the time. He didn't want noise. He didn't want chaos. Iritado.[5]

By the fourth day, he was back to normal. He'd wake up early and join me in taking his Ate Kala to school and picking her up at the end of the day. When they got home, he'd play with her. As soon as he got tired, he'd switch to his most-loved pastime: slouching on the sofa and watching his favourite children's show.

Aside from seeing them every Saturday or pay day, I'd call my children every morning and afternoon. And most of the time, Rebo was standing by to pick up the phone. But when the 'three days of suffering' in chemotherapy arrived, it was sheer luck that he was in a mood to talk to me. I would often ask him if he felt better and he would loudly answer, *'Magaying na!'* [I feel better!] I would also make him promise that he wouldn't leave me and his sister Kala, to which he often said, *'Ayoo na!'* [I don't want to!] Yet sometimes, he'd joke about it: *'Us-o o na!'* [I really want to!] Then, he'd sing a song he had learnt from TV.

If he only knew how disheartened I was to hear *'Us-o o na!'*, how my stomach turned from this premonition.

Just like other children, Rebo was excited about Christmas. December had just begun when he asked me to buy new clothes and toys. Before these gifts could even arrive, in the middle of December, we were shocked by the results of his new blood tests: cancer relapse. The cancer blasts had reappeared. He

---

[5] Irritated with emphasis on the Spanish suffix -tado (can be a noun, a state of mind, or an adjective).

needed to undergo the same chemotherapy again. Everything we had done in the past was for naught.

A new set of things to worry about—suffering, fatigue, donation drives, and hospital bills. Back to zero. Cancer cells from the first chemo regenerated and multiplied. His body would have to go through all of the treatments again after already being so worn out by the disease. I knew he wouldn't let it overwhelm him. Three days before the end of January, I answered his wish: '*Uwi na 'ayo 'tay! Ayaw o na a uspi-al! Di o na aya.*' [Let us go home, Tay. I don't want to be in the hospital anymore. I can't take it anymore.]

* * *

It weighed heavily on my chest.

The truth is that his mother and her relatives told me to leave the fate of Rebo in God's hands. I remember losing my temper over their arguments. It was the most defeatist, stupid, and faint-hearted argument I had ever heard. I yelled at them. Started a quarrel. But when Rebo spoke, I stopped. Even though I wanted to continue to fight, I told the doctors to stop the treatments because his body couldn't take it anymore. That was clear from the bruises that appeared across his body when we were just starting the first sessions of chemo.

My warrior fought for fourteen sessions and eleven months of treatment.

* * *

'Son, what do you want? A birthday party tomorrow? It's in five months, ah! But all right, if that's what you want. Yellow balloons? All yellow? Sure, I'll buy those. We'll prepare food because it's your birthday! Yippee!'

On the first Saturday after he got out of chemo, he wanted to throw a party in advance of his fifth birthday. I invited many people and asked them to bring gifts. It should be the best Saturday of all Saturdays. Toys everywhere. Stuffed animals, mini-helicopters, walkie-talkies, Crush Gear, remote-controlled cars, and most of all, his favourite, the Beyblade. Lots and lots of Beyblades.

He accepted all of it, and many other gifts for turning five. Even as an illusion. Even though it was not yet the time.

At the advance birthday party, he had a Beyblade tournament with his cousins.

Three days before the third Saturday, I came for a surprise visit. He was slowly losing strength. He didn't smile often anymore. He couldn't even move to launch the Beyblade on the floor so he held onto it in his frail hands. Sometimes he kept it in his pocket. But he tried to be strong even though he could no longer stand on his legs. He had blood clots inside his gums. Outside their home, I was very astonished when he asked, '*Tay, may pera a?*' [Tay, do you have any money?] I quickly pulled out my wallet, opened it, and showed him the cash crammed inside. I asked him what he wanted to buy, and he pointed to the nearby sari-sari store. No sooner had I bought the candies he asked for than he left the store and sat on the sidewalk. He was showing his fondness for me. Buying those candies was his way of showing his love for me. When we went back inside the house, ants swarmed over the untouched sweets on the pavement.

By the third Saturday, Rebo had lost all his hair. But it had not fallen out on its own. When he was irritated, he had pulled at his hair to completely remove it by the roots. On that day, I asked a favour from a colleague at work: to hire a mascot who would perform a free private show for Rebo. Though I didn't see him smile or laugh, I knew he was happy at the end of the show. It's the kind of happiness that slowly fades and disappears.

His strength waned in a flash, so by the fourth Saturday he couldn't even insert the ripcord inside the Beyblade launcher. When he spoke, he felt tired and gasped for breath. I tried taking him to the carnival but he only wanted to ride the Red Baron, a small helicopter that goes up and down, and rotates around an octopus. Whenever the ride went up, he'd look at me and smile with sadness in his eyes. After the ride, he asked to go home at once. And when we arrived, he immediately went to bed and stared at the blank ceiling.

The fifth Saturday was the last Saturday of February, exactly the end of the month. And at the end of February, my son died. It was only a matter of time after his tears had fallen before his glassy eyes closed, and he breathed his last breath.

He died in my arms. They told me that he waited for me before he died. We weren't able to talk anymore because by the time I arrived at the door, he was already screaming in agony.

He suffered for an hour and a half. Blind eyes, stiff body, mouth full of blood, and gasping breaths. 'This isn't true! I don't believe it. My son will live! He promised us he wouldn't leave me and his Ate Kala! Where's the peaceful death you all told me about?!' I wanted to shout all of this to the family around me but I wasn't able to speak. The grief was loud enough to silence me.

As someone who wanted to be a good father, when I knew he couldn't fight it anymore, I gently kissed him and let him go. 'Go ahead 'Bo. Thank you for the four years. We love you. Goodbye.'

And I cried and cried.

* * *

I won't be able to bring him to his first day of school anymore. We won't ever have those little heart-to-heart talks between a father and a son. Or even talk over beer about dating a girl. Or even argue or debate. Or travel somewhere.

What would have been his dreams even if he only lived for four years in this world? How about Kala? They were the closest allies when the separation happened. How can I explain to my firstborn that she wouldn't even see her brother again? That Rebo's loss means no one will be taking her to or picking her up from school. His clothes will miss him. His shoes will miss him. His books and toys will miss him. His sister, mother, and I will yearn for him.

I forbade the Beyblades to miss him, so I put all of them inside a white bag and placed it on top of his cold, blue hands before his coffin was lowered into the ground and the earth covered his grave.

It was the sixth Saturday when Rebo left the hospital. It was the last Saturday his loved ones saw him.

The Beyblade and their owner are gone now, laid to rest in the coffin. They journey into the afterlife, where there is no sickness, no hunger, and no suffering. Peacefully gyrating and turning. Spinning endlessly in bliss.

Meanwhile, those of us left behind grieving on earth will continue to survive and learn the art of grief.

Translator's Note

For National Artist for Literature Gemino H. Abad to translate is 'to carry the world over the language, to ferry across the words of the language, the wonder of nature, the miracle of living.'[6]

So to speak, it's like you're leaving on a jet plane or riding a bus somewhere, bringing with you yourself, your world, memories, and life to another time, place, and world. Abad likes to compare it to writing. When one writes, it's like somebody is translating if we ponder about it. We carry the idioms, deep thoughts, and world views of one culture to another medium, space, or form. With it, we also carry the culture's meaning and emotions. Like water that you transfer to a cup or a bowl, depending on what kind of shape or space that water will be filled, it will still be water. I do believe that Abad's words hold water in how I translated the ten pieces in *Six Saturdays of Beyblade and Other Essays*.

This was a labour of love, an act I carried like a child for months (to count from the year I started to the year I ended, it was nine months!), born out of the need to create and make sense of the world I was living in at the time I began writing it. I realized it was 2021, the Philippines was still in the middle of a pandemic. I thought at that time, life would end sooner, why not translate one of the celebrated essays in the country to be

---

[6] Dr Gemino Abad, 'Teaching Philippine Literature in English', UP Open University, *YouTube*, 21 January 2019.

129

read by the world? I wanted the people of the world to know that we have lots of very talented essayists in Filipino and their readership should transcend the boundaries that separate all of us in this world. If we were forced by colonialism to read Western writers, why can't we be read by those outside our country? And I think, lots of people are missing out on the good works done by Filipino writers in this country, especially those that try to challenge their writing style in the language of the streets.

So in 2022, when I was beginning to translate the title piece of the collection, *Six Saturdays of Beyblade*, I was imagining the moment I first fell in love with Jarin's prose in a creative writing class we were doing with my mentor Dr Luna Sicat-Cleto way back before the pandemic. I was in awe of the roughness of language. How was this guy able to write such coherence amidst the very messy language of the streets? Honestly, it had lots of fragments and run-ons but people loved it! The young people bought it, it sold out its first copies, it had another sell-out, and it was reprinted in the middle of the pandemic, with again a bestseller status. What was in that book? And what was in that essay? It was then that I realized people loved it because it was all about love.

Yes, you've heard it correctly. It wasn't tautology. This whole book is dedicated to love, as an afterword or an aftereffect. It is the love of a father to his dying son, the love of a friend to his unexpected friends, the love of a son to his struggling mom, the love of a grandchild to his grandparents, the love of a lover to his long lost lovers, the love of a colleague to a colleague. It was all about love at the end of the day. Like love, memories and translations don't end with the final word. It keeps on coming back on days we don't expect it. Isn't that how we remember flashbulb memories? Or perhaps, we contemplate the good old days, when we listen to music or smell something familiar, and we go with the flow of that wisp of a memory. I believe that the book must be read by many people across the world for it is a work of memory. It is also a guidebook to Philippine culture. Who would have thought that the Philippines have lots of words related to food, fishes, drinks, and instruments that can be translated to the global language? These essays are filled with Filipino culture; you'll never get the hang of it! More so, what Ferdinand Pisigan Jarin weaves in this collection of his personal essays are the things that ordinary people experience in their lives. Yet, he elevates it to a work of art and touches upon the hearts of those who might be going through a similar struggle in life. He didn't write it out of the need to win an award or get attention. He wasn't navel gazing just to chase a clout. Jarin wrote because he wanted to remember these epitaphs of people gone in his life and how they have shaped him as the person he is today. I think that's the work of memoir, to make somebody realize what has changed from when one began writing it to when one finished it. And oh boy, he learnt a lot. In a way, we too realized something in ourselves.

I began translating this collection in the middle of a pandemic, my father died of a heart attack, I lost my job, and I was writing in isolation. I never thought that I would be able to finish this project. What only made sense to me at that time was that to make sense of loss, I had to translate. Only God knows how hard it was to pull myself out of that rock bottom. However, what kept me going was the love of literature. I love the words written here. I love how it rings and makes you tear along the way. Sometimes you'll laugh and sometimes you'll get inspired. Though I must admit at times, it might be called tough love, for many of his words in the original Filipino or even the Sambal dialect were hard to translate. But the lesson that Jarin kept on reminding me as a translator is to keep the emotions intact, to make somebody feel what it is in the original and what it must have been to experience that memory. I was writing with a painful heart and a renewed soul. I lost love along the way, many of whom will not be able to read this collection anymore, but I yearn that one day, somebody they know might pick up this book, and tell the stories they've read here. The force that kept me going were these characters that I felt were very alive as I was writing them. Somehow I tend to compare them to the figures of a family that I might have once had in my life. The pandemic heightened that reality, that all the people we love, our friends and family will one day be gone and we will be left alone to ponder, or maybe if we had the extra time, write it at all. Write the good and the bad, and learn from it, the hard way.

The truth is this collection is all about Jarin. It's his trials and tribulations, his ups and downs, his ins and outs, his good days and bad days. But whenever he ends that trial, that journey, a topsy-turvy adventure from the far-flung countryside to the dirty street ways and alleys of Manila, he always finds a glimmer of light. Whatever that light is, I hope dear reader that you also find it in these stories. It is after all written to inspire and touch upon your lives, and maybe perhaps in the end, change a little bit about what you know about the world.

It is after all about love and so I end this note with the hope that you, dear reader, will find something about love and resilience in these essays. For what does the world need right now except the enduring act of love that we Filipinos are known for. Romantic? Nah. Sentimental? Maybe. But loving? Of course. This is what it means to translate an essay. It is an act of love, that image of Rebo, Jarin's son, playing the Beyblade in the covers whenever I'd go back and forth to check on the context of a phrase, a word, or a sentence. It is an act of love because a kid loves to play a spinning Beyblade, like life that goes around and comes back around. It is a joy captured in a photograph that will forever remind us of his death but also his father's love. It is an act of love, critical, filial, national, imaginary, enduring, whatever you call it.

Acknowledgements

First, I would like to thank Penguin Random House Southeast Asia for taking up this project and believing in the power of this translation.

My heartfelt thanks also to Dr Bassam Sidiki and his team of editors for believing in my translation, who first read and published it. The 'Six Saturdays of Beyblade' first came out in the Winter 2021 issue of the *Asymptote Journal*, an online journal dedicated to world translations.

I would also like to thank my creative writing mentor at the University of the Philippines, Dr Luna Sicat-Cleto, a trailblazing woman who needs to be known across the world for her feminist writing. Thank you Ma'am for introducing me to this collection way back in 2016 and for all that you have taught in the craft of writing.

Most of all, I'd like to thank Ferdinand Pisigan Jarin for believing and trusting me with his collection. This is my act of gratitude for your enduring work in creative nonfiction in the Philippines.

To Sean and Rod who saw this finish with me, thank you my hearts.

To Mama and Nanay for supporting me even though I almost gave up.

To Papa, whose absence was the force that pushed me to make this work happen.

And to you, dear reader, for finishing this book, with love.